THE OLD MERCHANT MARINE

THE CALIFORNIA CLIPPER SHIP, "FLYING CLOUD"

Lithograph, 1852. In the collection of the Bostonian Society, Old
State House, Boston

THE OLD
MERCHANT MARINE

A CHRONICLE OF
AMERICAN SHIPS AND SAILORS
BY RALPH D. PAINE

Fredonia Books
Amsterdam. The Netherlands

The Old Merchant Marine:
A Chronicle of American Ships and Sailors

by
Ralph D. Paine

ISBN: 1-58963-318-0

Copyright © 2001 by Fredonia Books

Reprinted from the 1919 edition

Fredonia Books
Amsterdam, The Netherlands
http://www.fredoniabooks.com

In order to make original editions of historical works
available to scholars at an economical price, this
facsimile of the original edition of 1919 is
reproduced from the best available copy and has
been digitally enhanced to improve legibility, but the
text remains unaltered to retain historical
authenticity.

CONTENTS

ILLUSTRATIONS

ix

THE OLD MERCHANT MARINE

CHAPTER I

COLONIAL ADVENTURERS IN LITTLE SHIPS

THE story of American ships and sailors is an epic of blue water which seems singularly remote, almost unreal, to the later generations. A people with a native genius for seafaring won and held a brilliant supremacy through two centuries and then forsook this heritage of theirs. The period of achievement was no more extraordinary than was its swift declension. A maritime race whose topsails flecked every ocean, whose captains courageous from father to son had fought with pike and carronade to defend the freedom of the seas, turned inland to seek a different destiny and took no more thought for the tall ships and rich cargoes which had earned so much renown for its flag.

Vanished fleets and brave memories — a chronicle of America which had written its closing chapters before the Civil War! There will be other Yankee merchantmen in times to come, but never days like those when skippers sailed on seas uncharted in quest of ports mysterious and unknown.

The Pilgrim Fathers, driven to the northward of their intended destination in Virginia, landed on the shore of Cape Cod not so much to clear the forest and till the soil as to establish a fishing settlement. Like the other Englishmen who long before 1620 had steered across to harvest the cod on the Grand Bank, they expected to wrest a livelihood mostly from salt water. The convincing argument in favor of Plymouth was that it offered a good harbor for boats and was "a place of profitable fishing." Both pious and amphibious were these pioneers whom the wilderness and the red Indian confined to the water's edge, where they were soon building ships to trade corn for beaver skins with the Kennebec colony.

Even more energetic in taking profit from the sea were the Puritans who came to Massachusetts Bay in 1629, bringing carpenters and shipbuilders with them to hew the pine and oak so close at hand into keelsons, frames, and planking. Two years later, Governor John Winthrop launched his thirty-ton sloop *Blessing of the Bay*, and sent her to open "friendly commercial relations" with the Dutch of Manhattan. Brisk though the traffic was in furs and wampum, these mariners of Boston and Salem were not content to voyage coastwise. Offshore fishing made skilled, adventurous seamen of them, and what they caught with hook and line, when dried and salted, was readily exchanged for other merchandise in Bermuda, Barbados, and Europe.

A vessel was a community venture, and the custom still survives in the ancient ports of the Maine coast where the shapely wooden schooners are fashioned. The blacksmith, the rigger, the calker, took their pay in shares. They became part owners, as did likewise the merchant who supplied stores and material; and when the ship was afloat, the master, the mates, and even the seamen, were allowed cargo space for commodities which they might buy and sell to their own advantage. Thus early they learned to trade as shrewdly as they navigated, and every voyage directly concerned a whole neighborhood.

This kind of enterprise was peculiar to New England because other resources were lacking. To the westward the French were more interested in exploring the rivers leading to the region of the Great Lakes and in finding fabulous rewards in furs. The Dutch on the Hudson were similarly engaged by means of the western trails to the country of the Iroquois, while the planters of Virginia had discovered an easy opulence in the tobacco crop, with slave labor to toil for them, and they were not compelled to turn to the hardships and the hazards of the sea. The New Englander, hampered by an unfriendly climate, hard put to it to grow sufficient food, with land immensely difficult to clear, was between the devil and the deep sea, and he sagaciously chose the latter. Elsewhere in the colonies the forest was an enemy to be destroyed with infinite pains. The New England pioneer regarded it with favor as the stuff with which to make stout ships and step the straight masts in them.

And so it befell that the seventeenth century had not run its course before New England was hardly afloat on every Atlantic trade route, causing Sir Josiah Child, British merchant and economist, to lament in 1668 that in his opinion nothing was "more prejudicial and in prospect more dangerous to any mother kingdom than the increase of shipping in her colonies, plantations, or provinces."

This absorbing business of building wooden vessels was scattered in almost every bay and river of the indented coast from Nova Scotia to Buzzard's Bay and the sheltered waters of Long Island Sound. It was not restricted, as now, to well-equipped yards with crews of trained artisans. Hard by the huddled hamlet of log houses was the row of keel-blocks sloping to the tide. In winter weather too rough for fishing, when the little farms lay idle, this Yankee Jack-of-all-trades plied his axe and adze to shape the timbers, and it was a routine task to peg together a sloop, a ketch, or a brig, mere cockle-shells, in which to fare forth to London, or Cadiz, or the Windward Islands — some of them not much larger and far less seaworthy than the lifeboat which hangs at a liner's davits. Pinching poverty forced him to dispense with the ornate, top-heavy cabins and forecastles of the foreign merchantmen, while invention, bred of necessity, molded finer lines and less clumsy models to weather the risks of a stormy coast and channels beset with shoals and ledges. The square-rig did well enough for deep-water voyages, but it was an awkward, lubberly contrivance for working along shore, and the colonial Yankee therefore evolved the schooner with her flat fore-and-aft sails which enabled her to beat to windward and which required fewer men in the handling.

Dimly but unmistakably these canny seafarers in their rude beginnings foreshadowed the creation of a merchant marine which should one day comprise the noblest, swiftest ships driven by the wind and the finest sailors that ever trod a deck. Even then these early vessels were conspicuously efficient, carrying smaller crews than the Dutch or English, paring expenses to a closer margin, daring to go wherever commerce beckoned in order to gain a dollar at peril of their skins.

By the end of the seventeenth century more than a thousand vessels were registered as built in the New England colonies, and Salem already displayed the peculiar talent for maritime adventure which was to make her the most illustrious port of the New World. The first of her line of shipping merchants was Philip English, who was sailing his own ketch *Speedwell* in 1676 and so rapidly advanced his fortunes that in a few years he was the richest man on the coast, with twenty-one vessels which traded coastwise with Virginia and offshore with Bilbao, Barbados, St. Christopher's, and France. Very devout were his bills of lading, flavored in this manner: "Twenty hogsheads of salt, shipped by the Grace of God in the good sloop called the *Mayflower*. . . . and by God's Grace bound to Virginia or Merriland."

No less devout were the merchants who ordered their skippers to cross to the coast of Guinea and fill the hold with negroes to be sold in the West Indies before returning with sugar and molasses to Boston or Rhode Island. The slave-trade flourished from the very birth of commerce in Puritan New England and its golden gains and exotic voyages allured high-hearted lads from farm and counter. In 1640 the ship *Desire*, built at Marblehead, returned from the West Indies and "brought some cotton and tobacco and negroes, etc. from thence." Earlier than this the Dutch of Manhattan had employed black labor, and it was provided that the Incorporated West India Company should "allot to each Patroon twelve black men and women out of the Prizes in which Negroes should be found."

It was in the South, however, that this kind of labor was most needed and, as the trade increased, Virginia and the Carolinas became the most lucrative markets. Newport and Bristol drove a roaring traffic in "rum and niggers," with a hundred sail to be found in the infamous Middle Passage. The master of one of these Rhode Island slavers, writing home from Guinea in 1736, portrayed the congestion of the trade in this wise: "For never was there so much Rum on the Coast at one time before. Not ye like of ye French ships was never seen before, for ye whole coast is full of them. For my part I can give no guess when I shall get away, for I purchast but 27 slaves since I have been here, for slaves is very scarce. We have had nineteen Sail of us at one time in ye Road, so that ships that used to carry pryme slaves off is now forced to take any that comes. Here is seven sail of us Rum men that are ready to devour one another, for our case is desprit."

Two hundred years of wickedness unspeakable and human torture beyond all computation, justified by Christian men and sanctioned by governments, at length rending the nation asunder in civil war and bequeathing a problem still unsolved — all this followed in the wake of those first voyages in search of labor which could be bought and sold as merchandise. It belonged to the dark ages with piracy and witchcraft, better forgotten than recalled, save for its potent influence in schooling brave seamen and building faster ships for peace and war.

These colonial seamen, in truth, fought for survival amid dangers so manifold as to make their hardihood astounding. It was not merely a matter of small vessels with a few men and boys daring distant voyages and the mischances of foundering or stranding, but of facing an incessant plague of privateers, French and Spanish, Dutch and English, or a swarm of freebooters under no flag at all. Coasts were unlighted, charts few and unreliable, and the instruments of navigation almost as crude as in the days of Columbus. Even the savage Indian, not content with lurking in ambush, went afloat to wreak mischief, and the records of the First Church of Salem contain this quaint entry under date of July 25, 1677: "The Lord having given a Commission to the Indians to take no less than 13 of the Fishing Ketches of Salem and Captivate the men . . . it struck a great consternation into all the people here. The Pastor moved on the Lord's Day, and the whole people readily consented, to keep the Lecture Day following as a Fast Day, which was accordingly done. . . . The Lord was pleased to send in some of the Ketches on the Fast Day which was looked on as a gracious smile of Providence. Also there had been 19 wounded men sent into Salem a little while before; also a Ketch sent out from Salem as a man-of-war to recover the rest of the Ketches. The Lord give them Good Success."

To encounter a pirate craft was an episode almost commonplace and often more sordid than picturesque. Many of these sea rogues were thieves with small stomach for cutlasses and slaughter. They were of the sort that overtook Captain John Shattuck sailing home from Jamaica in 1718 when he reported his capture by one Captain Charles Vain, "a Pyrat" of 12 guns and 120 men who took him to Crooked Island, plundered him of various articles, stripped the brig, abused the crew, and finally let him go. In the same year the seamen of the *Hopewell* related that near Hispaniola they met with pirates who robbed and ill-treated them and carried off their mate because they had no navigator.

Ned Low, a gentleman rover of considerable notoriety, stooped to filch the stores and gear from a fleet of fourteen poor fishermen off Cape Sable. He had a sense of dramatic values, however, and frequently brandished his pistols on deck, besides which, as set down by one of his prisoners, "he had a young child in Boston for whom he entertained such tenderness that on every lucid interval from

drinking and revelling, I have seen him sit down
and weep plentifully."

A more satisfying figure was Thomas Pounds,
who was taken by the sloop *Mary*, sent after him
from Boston in 1689. He was discovered in Vine-
yard Sound, and the two vessels fought a gallant
action, the pirate flying a red flag and refusing
to strike. Captain Samuel Pease of the *Mary*
was mortally wounded, while Pounds, this proper pirate, strode his quarter-deck and waved his
naked sword, crying, "Come on board, ye dogs,
and I will strike *you* presently." This invitation
was promptly accepted by the stout seamen from
Boston, who thereupon swarmed over the bulwark
and drove all hands below, preserving Thomas
Pounds to be hanged in public.

In 1703 John Quelch, a man of resource, hoisted
what he called "Old Roger" over the *Charles* — a
brigantine which had been equipped as a privateer
to cruise against the French of Acadia. This curious flag of his was described as displaying a skele-
ton with an hour-glass in one hand and "a dart
in the heart with three drops of blood proceeding from it in the other." Quelch led a mutiny,
tossed the skipper overboard, and sailed for Brazil,
capturing several merchantmen on the way and

looting them of rum, silks, sugar, gold dust, and munitions. Rashly he came sailing back to Marblehead, primed with a plausible yarn, but his men talked too much when drunk and all hands were jailed. Upon the gallows Quelch behaved exceedingly well, "pulling off his hat and bowing to the spectators," while the somber Puritan merchants in the crowd were, many of them, quietly dealing in the merchandise fetched home by pirates who were lucky enough to steer clear of the law.

This was a shady industry in which New York took the more active part, sending out supplies to the horde of pirates who ravaged the waters of the Far East and made their haven at Madagascar, and disposing of the booty received in exchange. Governor Fletcher had dirtied his hands by protecting this commerce and, as a result, Lord Bellomont was named to succeed him. Said William III, "I send you, my Lord, to New York, because an honest and intrepid man is wanted to put these abuses down, and because I believe you to be such a man."

Such were the circumstances in which Captain William Kidd, respectable master mariner in the merchant service, was employed by Lord Bellomont, royal Governor of New York, New Hampshire, and

Massachusetts, to command an armed ship and harry the pirates of the West Indies and Madagascar. Strangest of all the sea tales of colonial history is that of Captain Kidd and his cruise in the *Adventure-Galley*. His name is reddened with crimes never committed, his grisly phantom has stalked through the legends and literature of piracy, and the Kidd tradition still has magic to set treasure-seekers exploring almost every beach, cove, and headland from Halifax to the Gulf of Mexico. Yet if truth were told, he never cut a throat or made a victim walk the plank. He was tried and hanged for the trivial offense of breaking the head of a mutinous gunner of his own crew with a wooden bucket. It was even a matter of grave legal doubt whether he had committed one single piratical act. His trial in London was a farce. In the case of the captured ships he alleged that they were sailing under French passes, and he protested that his privateering commission justified him, and this contention was not disproven. The suspicion is not wanting that he was condemned as a scapegoat because certain noblemen of England had subscribed the capital to outfit his cruise, expecting to win rich dividends in gold captured from the pirates he was sent to

attack. Against these men a political outcry was
raised, and as a result Captain Kidd was sacrificed.
He was a seaman who had earned honorable dis-
tinction in earlier years, and fate has played his
memory a shabby trick.

It was otherwise with Blackbeard, most flam-
boyant of all colonial pirates who filled the stage
with swaggering success, chewing wine-glasses in
his cabin, burning sulphur to make his ship seem
more like hell, and industriously scourging the
whole Atlantic coast. Charleston lived in terror
of him until Lieutenant Maynard, in a small sloop,
laid him alongside in a hammer-and-tongs engagement and cut off the head of Blackbeard to dangle
from the bowsprit as a trophy.

Of this rudely adventurous era, it would be hard
to find a seaman more typical than the redoubta-
ble Sir William Phips who became the first royal Governor of the Massachusetts Colony in 1692.
Born on a frontier farm of the Maine coast while
many of the Pilgrim fathers were living, "his faithful mother," wrote Cotton Mather, "had no less
than twenty-six children, whereof twenty-one were
sons; but equivalent to them all was William, one
of the youngest, whom, his father dying, was left
young with his mother, and with her he lived,

keeping ye sheep in ye Wilderness until he was
eighteen years old." Then he apprenticed himself
to a neighboring shipwright who was building
sloops and pinnaces and, having learned the trade,
set out for Boston. As a ship-carpenter he plied
his trade, spent his wages in the taverns of the
waterside and there picked up wondrous yarns
of the silver-laden galleons of Spain which had
shivered their timbers on the reefs of the Bahama
Passage or gone down in the hurricanes that beset
those southerly seas. Meantime he had married a
wealthy widow whose property enabled him to go
treasure-hunting on the Spanish main. From his
first voyage thither in a small vessel he escaped
with his life and barely enough treasure to pay the
cost of the expedition.

In no wise daunted he laid his plans to search
for a richly ladened galleon which was said to have
been wrecked half a century before off the coast of
Hispaniola. Since his own funds were not sufficient
for this exploit, he betook himself to England to
enlist the aid of the Government. With bulldog
persistence he besieged the court of James II for
a whole year, this rough-and-ready New England
shipmaster, until he was given a royal frigate for
his purpose. He failed to fish up more silver from

the sands but, nothing daunted, he persuaded other patrons to outfit him with a small merchantman, the *James and Mary*, in which he sailed for the coast of Hispaniola. This time he found his galleon and thirty-two tons of silver. "Besides that incredible treasure of plate, thus fetched up from seven or eight fathoms under water, there were vast riches of Gold, and Pearls, and Jewels. . . . All that a Spanish frigot was to be enriched withal."

Up the Thames sailed the lucky little merchantman in the year of 1687, with three hundred thousand pounds sterling as her freightage of treasure. Captain Phips made honest division with his backers and, because men of his integrity were not over plentiful in England after the Restoration, King James knighted him. He sailed home to Boston, "a man of strong and sturdy frame," as Hawthorne fancied him, "whose face had been roughened by northern tempests and blackened by the burning sun of the West Indies. . . . He wears an immense periwig flowing down over his shoulders. . . . His red, rough hands which have done many a good day's work with the hammer and adze are half-covered by the delicate lace ruffles at the wrist." But he carried with him the manners of the forecastle, a man hasty and unlettered but superbly brave and honest. Even after he had become Governor he thrashed the captain of the *Nonesuch* frigate of the royal navy, and used his fists on the Collector of the Port after cursing him with tremendous gusto. Such behavior in a Governor was too strenuous, and Sir William Phips was summoned to England, where he died while waiting his restoration to office and royal favor. Failing both, he dreamed of still another treasure voyage, "for it was his purpose, upon his dismission from his Government once more to have gone upon his old Fishing-Trade, upon a mighty shelf of rock and banks of sand that lie where he had informed himself."

CHAPTER II

THE wars of England with France and Spain spread turmoil upon the high seas during the greater part of the eighteenth century. Yet with an immense tenacity of purpose, these briny forefathers increased their trade and multiplied their ships in the face of every manner of adversity. The surprising fact is that most of them were not driven ashore to earn their bread. What Daniel Webster said of them at a later day was true from the beginning: "It is not, sir, by protection and bounties, but by unwearied exertion, by extreme economy, by that manly and resolute spirit which relies on itself to protect itself. These causes alone enable American ships still to keep the element and show the flag of their country in distant seas."

What was likely to befall a shipmaster in the turbulent eighteenth century may be inferred from the misfortunes of Captain Michael Driver of

Salem. In 1759 he was in command of the schooner *Three Brothers*, bound to the West Indies on his lawful business. Jogging along with a cargo of fish and lumber, he was taken by a privateer under British colors and sent into Antigua as a prize. Unable to regain either his schooner or his two thousand dollar cargo, he sadly took passage for home. Another owner gave him employment and he set sail in the schooner *Betsy* for Guadaloupe. During this voyage, poor man, he was captured and carried into port by a French privateer. On the suggestion that he might ransom his vessel on payment of four thousand livres, he departed for Boston in hope of finding the money, leaving behind three of his sailors as hostages.

Cash in hand for the ransom, the long-suffering Captain Michael Driver turned southward again, now in the schooner *Mary*, and he flew a flag of truce to indicate his errand. This meant nothing to the ruffian who commanded the English privateer *Revenge*. He violently seized the innocent *Mary* and sent her into New Providence. Here Captain Driver made lawful protest before the authorities, and was set at liberty with vessel and cargo — an act of justice quite unusual in the Admiralty Court of the Bahamas.

Unmolested, the harassed skipper managed to gain Cape François and rescue his three seamen and his schooner in exchange for the ransom money. As he was about to depart homeward bound, a French frigate snatched him and his crew out of their vessel and threw them ashore at Santiago, where for two months they existed as ragged beachcombers until by some judicial twist the schooner was returned to them. They worked her home and presented their long list of grievances to the colonial Government of Massachusetts, which duly forwarded them — and that was the end of it. Three years had been spent in this catalogue of misadventures, and Captain Driver, his owners, and his men were helpless against such intolerable aggression. They and their kind were a prey to every scurvy rascal who misused a privateering commission to fill his own pockets.

Stoutly resolved to sail and trade as they pleased, these undaunted Americans, nevertheless, increased their business on blue water until shortly before the Revolution the New England fleet alone numbered six hundred sail. Its captains felt at home in Surinam and the Canaries. They trimmed their yards in the reaches of the Mediterranean and the North Sea or bargained thriftily in the Levant.

The whalers of Nantucket, in their apple-bowed barks, explored and hunted in distant seas, and the smoke of their try-pots darkened the waters of Baffin Bay, Guinea, and Brazil. It was they who inspired Edmund Burke's familiar eulogy: "No sea but is vexed by their fisheries. No climate that is not a witness to their toils. Neither the perseverance of Holland nor the activity of France, nor the dexterous and firm sagacity of England ever carried this most perilous mode of hardy industry to the extent to which it has been pushed by this recent people — a people who are still, as it were, but in the gristle and not yet hardened into the bone of manhood."

In 1762, seventy-eight whalers cleared from American ports, of which more than half were from Nantucket. Eight years later there were one hundred and twenty-five whalers out of Nantucket which took 14,331 barrels of oil valued at $358,200. In size these vessels averaged no more than ninety tons, a fishing smack of today, and yet they battered their way half around the watery globe and comfortably supported six thousand people who dwelt on a sandy island unfit for farming and having no other industries. Every Nantucket lad sailed for his "lay" or share of the catch and aspired to command eventually a whaler of his own.

Whaler, merchantman, and slaver were training a host of incomparable seamen destined to harry the commerce of England under the new-born Stars and Stripes, and now, in 1775, on the brink of actual war, Parliament flung a final provocation and aroused the furious enmity of the fishermen who thronged the Grand Bank. Lord North proposed to forbid the colonies to export fish to those foreign markets in which every seacoast village was vitally concerned, and he also contemplated driving the fishing fleets from their haunts off Newfoundland. This was to rob six thousand sturdy men of a livelihood afloat and to spread ruin among the busy ports, such as Marblehead and Gloucester, from which sailed hundreds of pinks, snows, and schooners. This measure became law notwithstanding the protests of twenty-one peers of the realm who declared: "We dissent because the attempt to coerce by famine the whole body of the inhabitants of great and populous provinces is without example in the history of this, or perhaps, of any civilized nation."

The sailormen bothered their heads very little about taxation without representation but whetted

A WHALE SHIP ON THE NORTHWEST COAST, "CUTTING IN" HER LAST RIGHT WHALE

Lithograph. In the collection of the Bostonian Society, Old State House, Boston.

their anger with grudges more robust. They had been beggared and bullied and shot at from the Bay of Biscay to Barbados, and no sooner was the Continental Congress ready to issue privateering commissions and letters of marque than for them it was up anchor and away to bag a Britisher. Scarcely had a shipmaster signaled his arrival with a deep freight of logwood, molasses, or sugar than he received orders to discharge with all speed and clear his decks for mounting heavier batteries and slinging the hammocks of a hundred eager privateersmen who had signed articles in the tavern rendezvous. The timbered warehouses were filled with long-toms and nine-pounders, muskets, blunderbusses, pistols, cutlases, boarding-pikes, hand grenades, tomahawks, grape, canister, and double-headed shot.

In the narrow, gabled streets of Salem, Boston, New York, and Baltimore, crowds trooped after the fifes and drums with a strapping recruiting officer to enroll "all gentlemen seamen and able-bodied landsmen who had a mind to distinguish themselves in the glorious cause of their country and make their fortunes." Many a ship's company was mustered between noon and sunset, including men who had served in armed merchantmen and who in times of nominal peace had fought the marauders of Europe or whipped the corsairs of Barbary in the Strait of Gibraltar. Never was a race of seamen so admirably fitted for the daring trade of privateering as the crews of these tall sloops, topsail schooners, and smart square-riggers, their sides checkered with gun-ports, and ready to drive to sea like hawks.

In some instances the assurance of these hardy men was both absurd and sublime. Ramshackle boats with twenty or thirty men aboard, mounting one or two old guns, sallied out in the expectation of gold and glory, only to be captured by the first British cruiser that chanced to sight them. A few even sailed with no cannon at all, confident of taking them out of the first prize overhauled by laying alongside — and so in some cases they actually did.

The privateersmen of the Revolution played a larger part in winning the war than has been commonly recognized. This fact, however, was clearly perceived by Englishmen of that era, as *The London Spectator* candidly admitted: "The books at Lloyds will recount it, and the rate of assurances at that time will prove what their diminutive strength was able to effect in the face of our navy, and that when nearly one hundred pennants were flying on our coast. Were we able to prevent their going in and out, or stop them from taking our trade and our storeships even in sight of our garrisons? Besides, were they not in the English and Irish Channels, picking up our homeward bound trade, sending their prizes into French and Spanish ports to the great terror of our merchants and shipowners?"

The naval forces of the Thirteen Colonies were pitifully feeble in comparison with the mighty fleets of the enemy whose flaming broadsides upheld the ancient doctrine that "the Monarchs of Great Britain have a peculiar and Sovereign authority upon the Ocean . . . from the Laws of God and of Nature, besides an uninterrupted Fruition of it for so many Ages past as that its Beginnings cannot be traced out."[1]

In 1776 only thirty-one Continental cruisers of all classes were in commission, and this number was swiftly diminished by capture and blockade until in 1782 no more than seven ships flew the flag of the American Navy. On the other hand, at the close of 1777, one hundred and seventy-four private armed vessels had been commissioned, mounting

[1] *The Seaman's Vade-Mecum.*   London, 1744.

two thousand guns and carrying nine thousand men. During this brief period of the war they took as prizes 733 British merchantmen and inflicted losses of more than two million pounds sterling. Over ten thousand seamen were made prisoners at a time when England sorely needed them for drafting into her navy. To lose them was a far more serious matter than for General Washington to capture as many Hessian mercenaries who could be replaced by purchase.

In some respects privateering as waged a century and more ago was a sordid, unlovely business, the ruling motive being rather a greed of gain than an ardent love of country. Shares in lucky ships were bought and sold in the gambling spirit of a stock exchange. Fortunes were won and lost regardless of the public service. It became almost impossible to recruit men for the navy because they preferred the chance of booty in a privateer. For instance, the State of Massachusetts bought a twenty-gun ship, the *Protector*, as a contribution to the naval strength, and one of her crew, Ebenezer Fox, wrote of the effort to enlist sufficient men: "The recruiting business went on slowly, however, but at length upwards of three hundred men were carried, dragged, and driven abroad; of all ages, kinds,

and descriptions; in all the various stages of in-
toxication from that of sober tipsiness to beastly
drunkenness; with the uproar and clamor that
may be more easily imagined than described.
Such a motley group has never been seen since
Falstaff's ragged regiment paraded the streets of
Coventry."

There was nothing of glory to boast of in fetching into port some little Nova Scotia coasting
schooner with a cargo of deals and potatoes, whose
master was also the owner and who lost the savings
of a lifetime because he lacked the men and guns
to defend his property against spoliation. The
war was no concern of his, and he was the victim
of a system now obsolete among civilized nations,
a relic of a barbarous and piratical age whose spirit
has been revived and gloried in recently only by
the Government of the German Empire. The chief
fault of the privateersman was that he sailed and
fought for his own gain, but he was never guilty
of sinking ships with passengers and crew aboard,
and very often he played the gentleman in gallant
style. Nothing could have seemed to him more
abhorrent and incredible than a kind of warfare
which should drown women and children because
they had embarked under an enemy's flag.

Extraordinary as were the successes of the Yankee privateers, it was a game of give-and-take, a weapon which cut both ways, and the temptation is to extol their audacious achievements while glossing over the heavy losses which their own merchant marine suffered. The weakness of privateering was that it was wholly offensive and could not, like a strong navy, protect its own commerce from depredation. While the Americans were capturing over seven hundred British vessels during the first two years of the war, as many as nine hundred American ships were taken or sunk by the enemy, a rate of destruction which fairly swept the Stars and Stripes from the tracks of ocean commerce. As prizes these vessels were sold at Liverpool and London for an average amount of two thousand pounds each and the loss to the American owners was, of course, ever so much larger.

The fact remains, nevertheless — and it is a brilliant page of history to recall — that in an inchoate nation without a navy, with blockading squadrons sealing most of its ports, with ragged armies on land which retreated oftener than they fought, private armed ships dealt the maritime prestige of Great Britain a far deadlier blow than the Dutch, French, and Spanish were able to inflict. In England, there resulted actual distress, even lack of food, because these intrepid seamen could not be driven away from her own coasts and continued to snatch their prizes from under the guns of British forts and fleets. The plight of the West India Colonies was even worse, as witness this letter from a merchant of Grenada: "We are happy if we can get anything for money by reason of the quantity of vessels taken by the Americans. A fleet of vessels came from Ireland a few days ago. From sixty vessels that departed from Ireland not above twenty-five arrived in this and neighboring islands, the others, it is thought, being all taken by American privateers. God knows, if this American war continues much longer, we shall all die of hunger."

On both sides, by far the greater number of captures was made during the earlier period of the war which cleared the seas of the smaller, slower, and unarmed vessels. As the war progressed and the profits flowed in, swifter and larger ships were built for the special business of privateering until the game resembled actual naval warfare. Whereas, at first, craft of ten guns with forty or fifty men had been considered adequate for the service,

three or four years later ships were afloat with a
score of heavy cannon and a trained crew of a
hundred and fifty or two hundred men, ready to
engage a sloop of war or to stand up to the
enemy's largest privateers. In those days single
ship actions, now almost forgotten in naval tac-
tics, were fought with illustrious skill and courage, and commanders won victories worthy of
comparison with deeds distinguished in the annals
of the American Navy.

CHAPTER III

OUT CUTLASES AND BOARD!

SALEM was the foremost privateering port of the Revolution, and from this pleasant harbor, long since deserted by ships and sailormen, there filled away past Cape Ann one hundred and fifty-eight vessels of all sizes to scan the horizon for British topsails. They accounted for four hundred prizes, or half the whole number to the credit of American arms afloat. This preëminence was due partly to freedom from a close blockade and partly to a seafaring population which was born and bred to its trade and knew no other. Besides the crews of Salem merchantmen, privateering enlisted the idle fishermen of ports nearby and the mariners of Boston whose commerce had been snuffed out by the British occupation. Philadelphia, Baltimore, and Charleston sent some splendid armed ships to sea but not with the impetuous rush nor in anything like the numbers enrolled by this gray old town whose fame was unique.

For the most part, the records of all these brave ships and the thousands of men who sailed and sweated and fought in them are dim and scanty, no more than routine entries in dusty log-books which read like this: "Filled away in pursuit of a second sail in the N. W.   At 4.30 she hoisted English colors and commenced firing her stern guns. At 5.20 took in the steering sails, at the same time she fired a broadside.   We opened a fire from our larboard battery and at 5.30 she struck her colors. Got out the boats and boarded her.   She proved to be the British brig *Acorn* from Liverpool to Rio Janeiro, mounting fourteen cannon."[1]   But now and then one finds in these old sea-journals an entry more intimate and human, such as the complaint of the master of the privateer *Scorpion*, cruising in 1778 and never a prize in sight.   "This Book I made to keep the Accounts of my Voyage but God knows beste what that will be, for I am at this time very Impashent but I hope soon there will be a Change to ease my Trubled Mind.   On this Day I was Chaced by Two Ships of War which

---

[1] From the manuscript collections of the Essex Institute, Salem, Mass.

I tuck to be Enemies, but coming on thick Weather I have lost site of them and so conclude myself escaped which is a small good Fortune in the midste of my Discouragements."[1] A burst of gusty laughter still echoes along the crowded deck of the letter-of-marque schooner *Success*, whose master, Captain Philip Thrash, inserted this diverting comment in his humdrum record of the day's work: "At one half past 8 discovered a sail ahead. Tacked ship. At 9 tacked ship again and past just to Leeward of the Sail which appeared to be a damn'd Comical Boat, by G—d."[1]

There are a few figures of the time and place which stand out, full-length, in vivid colors against a background that satisfies the desire of romance and thrillingly conveys the spirit of the time and the place. Such a one was Captain Jonathan Haraden, Salem privateersman, who captured one thousand British cannon afloat and is worthy to be ranked as one of the ablest sea-fighters of his generation. He was a merchant mariner, a master at the outbreak of the Revolution, who had followed the sea since boyhood. But it was more to his taste to command the Salem ship *General*

[1] From the manuscript collections of the Essex Institute, Salem, Mass.

Pickering of 180 tons which was fitted out under
a letter of marque in the spring of 1780. She
carried fourteen six-pounders and forty-five men
and boys, nothing very formidable, when Captain
Haraden sailed for Bilbao with a cargo of sugar.
During the voyage, before his crew had been ham-
mered into shape, he beat off a British privateer
of twenty guns and safely tacked into the Bay
of Biscay.

There he sighted another hostile privateer, the
Golden Eagle, larger than his own ship. Instead of
shifting his course to avoid her, Haraden clapped
on sail and steered alongside after nightfall, roaring
through his trumpet: "What ship is this? An
American frigate, sir.   Strike, or I'll sink you with
a broadside."

Dazed by this unexpected summons in the gloom,
the master of the *Golden Eagle* promptly surrendered, and a prize crew was thrown aboard with
orders to follow the *Pickering* into Bilbao. While
just outside that Spanish harbor, a strange sail
was descried and again Jonathan Haraden cleared
for action.   The vessel turned out to be the *Achilles*,
one of the most powerful privateers out of London,
with forty guns and a hundred and fifty men, or
almost thrice the fighting strength of the little

Pickering. She was, in fact, more like a sloop of war. Before Captain Haraden could haul within gunshot to protect his prize, it had been recaptured by the *Achilles*, which then maneuvered to engage the *Pickering*.

Darkness intervened, but Jonathan Haraden had no idea of escaping under cover of it. He was waiting for the morning breeze and a chance to fight it out to a finish. He was a handsome man with an air of serene composure and a touch of the theatrical such as Nelson displayed in his great moments. Having prepared his ship for battle, he slept soundly until dawn and then dressed with fastidious care to stroll on deck, where he beheld the *Achilles* bearing down on him with her crew at quarters.

His own men were clustered behind their open ports, matches lighted, tackles and breechings cast off, crowbars, handspikes, and sponge-staves in place, gunners stripped to the waist, powder-boys ready for the word like sprinters on the mark. Forty-five of them against a hundred and fifty, and Captain Haraden, debonair, unruffled, walking to and fro with a leisurely demeanor, remarking that although the *Achilles* appeared to be superior in force, "he had no doubt they would beat her if

they were firm and steady and did not throw away
their fire."

It was, indeed, a memorable sea-picture, the
sturdy *Pickering* riding deep with her burden of
sugar and seeming smaller than she really was,
the *Achilles* towering like a frigate, and all Bilbao turned out to watch the duel, shore and headlands crowded with spectators, the blue harbor-
mouth gay with an immense flotilla of fishing-boats
and pleasure craft. The stake for which Haraden
fought was to retake the *Golden Eagle* prize and
to gain his port. His seamanship was flawless.
Vastly outnumbered if it should come to boarding,
he handled his vessel so as to avoid the *Achilles*
while he poured the broadsides into her. After
two hours the London privateer emerged from the
smoke which had obscured the combat and put
out to sea in flight, hulled through and through,
while a farewell flight of crowbars, with which
the guns of the *Pickering* had been crammed to
the muzzle, ripped through her sails and rigging.

Haraden hoisted canvas and drove in chase,
but the *Achilles* had the heels of him "with a mainsail as large as a ship of the line," and reluctantly
he wore ship and, with the *Golden Eagle* again in
his possession, he sailed to an anchorage in Bilbao

harbor. The Spanish populace welcomed him with
tremendous enthusiasm. He was carried through
the streets in a holiday procession and was the hero
of banquets and public receptions.

Such a man was bound to be the idol of his
sailors and one of them quite plausibly related that
"so great was the confidence he inspired that if he
but looked at a sail through his glass and told the
helmsman to steer for her, the observation went
round,'If she is an enemy, she is ours.'"

It was in this same *General Pickering*, no longer
sugar-laden but in cruising trim, that Jonathan
Haraden accomplished a feat which Paul Jones
might have been proud to claim. There lifted
above the sky-line three armed merchantmen sailing in company from Halifax to New York, a brig
of fourteen guns, a ship of sixteen guns, a sloop of
twelve guns. When they flew signals and formed
in line, the ship alone appeared to outmatch the
Pickering, but Haraden, in that lordly manner of
his, assured his men that "he had no doubt whatever that if they would do their duty he would
quickly capture the three vessels." Here was performance very much out of the ordinary, naval
strategy of an exceptionally high order, and yet
it is dismissed by the only witness who took the

trouble to mention it in these few, casual words: "This he did with great ease by going alongside of each of them, one after the other."

One more story of this master sea-rover of the Revolution, sailor and gentleman, who served his country so much more brilliantly than many a landsman lauded in the written histories of the war. While in the *Pickering* he attacked a heavily armed royal mail packet bound to England from the West Indies, one of the largest merchant vessels of her day and equipped to defend herself against privateers. A tough antagonist and a hard nut to crack! They battered each other like two pugilists for four hours and even then the decision was still in the balance. Then Haraden sheered off to mend his damaged gear and splintered hull before closing in again.

He then discovered that all his powder had been shot away excepting one last charge. Instead of calling it a drawn battle, he rammed home this last shot in the locker, and ran down to windward of the packet, so close that he could shout across to the other quarter-deck: "I will give you five minutes to haul down your colors. If they are not down at the end of that time, I will fire into you and sink you, so help me God."

It was the bluff magnificent — courage cold-blooded and calculating. The adversary was still unbeaten. Haraden stood with watch in hand and sonorously counted off the minutes. It was the stronger will and not the heavier metal that won the day. To be shattered by fresh broadsides at pistol-range was too much for the nerves of the gallant English skipper whose decks were already like a slaughterhouse. One by one, Haraden shouted the minutes and his gunners blew their matches. At "four" the red ensign came fluttering down and the mail packet was a prize of war.

Another merchant seaman of this muster-roll of patriots was Silas Talbot, who took to salt water as a cabin boy at the age of twelve and was a prosperous shipmaster at twenty-one with savings invested in a house of his own in Providence. Enlisting under Washington, he was made a captain of infantry and was soon promoted, but he was restless ashore and glad to obtain an odd assignment. As Colonel Talbot he selected sixty infantry volunteers, most of them seamen by trade, and led them aboard the small sloop *Argo* in May, 1779, to punish the New York Tories who were equipping privateers against their own countrymen and working great mischief in Long Island Sound. So serious was the situation that General Gates found it almost impossible to obtain food supplies for the northern department of the Continental army.

Silas Talbot and his nautical infantrymen promptly fell in with the New York privateer *Lively*, a fair match for him, and as promptly sent her into port. He then ran offshore and picked up and carried into Boston two English privateers headed for New York with large cargoes of merchandise from the West Indies. But he was particularly anxious to square accounts with a renegade Captain Hazard who made Newport his base and had captured many American vessels with the stout brig *King George*, using her for "the base purpose of plundering his old neighbors and friends."

On his second cruise in the *Argo*, young Silas Talbot encountered the perfidious *King George* to the southward of Long Island and riddled her with one broadside after another, first hailing Captain Hazard by name and cursing him in double-shotted phrases for the traitorous swab that he was. Then the seagoing infantry scrambled over the bulwarks and tumbled the Tories down their own hatches without losing a man. A prize crew with the humiliated *King George* made for New London, where there was much cheering in the port, and "even the women, both young and old, expressed the greatest joy."

With no very heavy fighting, Talbot had captured five vessels and was keen to show what his crew could do against mettlesome foemen. He found them at last well out to sea in a large ship which seemed eager to engage him. Only a few hundred feet apart through a long afternoon, they briskly and cheerily belabored each other with grape and solid shot. Talbot's speaking-trumpet was shot out of his hand, the tails of his coat were shorn off, and all the officers and men stationed with him on the quarter-deck were killed or wounded.

His crew reported that the *Argo* was in a sinking condition, with the water flooding the gun-deck, but he told them to lower a man or two in the bight of a line and they pluckily plugged the holes from overside. There was a lusty huzza when the Englishman's mainmast crashed to the deck and this finished the affair. Silas Talbot found that he had trounced the privateer *Dragon*, of twice his own tonnage and with the advantage in both guns and men.

While his crew was patching the *Argo* and pumping the water from her hold, the lookout yelled

that another sail was making for them. Without
hesitation Talbot somehow got this absurdly im-
pudent one-masted craft of his under way and told
those of his sixty men who survived to prepare
for a second tussle. Fortunately another Yankee
privateer joined the chase and together they sub-
dued the armed brig *Hannah*. When the *Argo*
safely convoyed the two prizes into New Bedford,
"all who beheld her were astonished that a vessel
of her diminutive size could suffer so much and yet
get safely to port."

Men fought and slew each other in those rude
and distant days with a certain courtesy, with a
fine, punctilious regard for the etiquette of the
bloody game. There was the Scotch skipper of
the *Betsy*, a privateer, whom Silas Talbot hailed as
follows, before they opened fire:

"You must now haul down those British colors,
my friend."

"Notwithstanding I find you an enemy, as I
suspected," was the dignified reply, "yet, sir, I
shall let them hang a little bit longer, — with your
permission, — so fire away, Flanagan."

During another of her cruises the *Argo* pursued an artfully disguised ship of the line which
could have blown her to kingdom come with

a broadside of thirty guns. The little *Argo* was actually becalmed within short range, but her company got out the sweeps and rowed her some distance before darkness and a favoring slant of wind carried them clear. In the summer of 1780, Captain Silas Talbot, again a mariner by title, was given the private cruiser *General Washington* with one hundred and twenty men, but he was less fortunate with her than when afloat in the tiny *Argo* with his sixty Continentals. Off Sandy Hook he ran into the British fleet under Admiral Arbuthnot and, being outsailed in a gale of wind, he was forced to lower his flag to the great seventy-four *Culloden*. After a year in English prisons he was released and made his way home, serving no more in the war but having the honor to command the immortal frigate *Constitution* in 1799 as a captain in the American Navy.

In several notable instances the privateersmen tried conclusions with ships that flew the royal ensign, and got the better of them. The hero of an uncommonly brilliant action of this sort was Captain George Geddes of Philadelphia, who was entrusted with the *Congress*, a noble privateer of twenty-four guns and two hundred men. Several of the smaller British cruisers had been sending parties ashore to plunder estates along the southern shores, and one of them, the sloop of war *Savage*, had even raided Washington's home at Mount Vernon. Later she shifted to the coast of Georgia in quest of loot and was unlucky enough to fall athwart Captain Geddes in the *Congress*.

The privateer was the more formidable ship and faster on the wind, forcing Captain Sterling of the *Savage* to accept the challenge. Disabled aloft very early in the fight, Captain Geddes was unable to choose his position, for which reason they literally battled hand-to-hand, hulls grinding against each other, the gunners scorched by the flashes of the cannon in the ports of the opposing ship, with scarcely room to ply the rammers, and the sailors throwing missiles from the decks, hand grenades, cold shot, scraps of iron, belaying-pins.

As the vessels lay interlocked, the *Savage* was partly dismasted and Captain Geddes, leaping upon the forecastle head, told the boarders to follow him. Before they could swing their cutlases and dash over the hammock-nettings, the British boatswain waved his cap and yelled that the *Savage* had surrendered. Captain Sterling was dead, eight others were killed, and twenty-four wounded. The American loss was about the

same. Captain Geddes, however, was unable to
save his prize because a British frigate swooped
down and took them both into Charleston.

When peace came in 1783, it was independence
dearly bought by land and sea, and no small part
of the price was the loss of a thousand merchant
ships which would see their home ports no more.
Other misfortunes added to the toll of destruction.
The great fishing fleets which had been the chief
occupation of coastwise New England were almost
obliterated and their crews were scattered. Many
of the men had changed their allegiance and were
sailing out of Halifax, and others were impressed
into British men-of-war or returned broken in
health from long confinement in British prisons.
The ocean was empty of the stanch schooners
which had raced home with lee rails awash to cheer
waiting wives and sweethearts.

The fate of Nantucket and its whalers was even
more tragic. This colony on its lonely island amid
the shoals was helpless against raids by sea, and
its ships and storehouses were destroyed without
mercy. Many vessels in distant waters were captured before they were even aware that a state
of war existed. Of a fleet numbering a hundred
and fifty sail, one hundred and thirty-four were

taken by the enemy and Nantucket whaling suffered almost total extinction. These seamen, thus robbed of their livelihood, fought nobly for their country's cause. Theirs was not the breed to sulk or whine in port. Twelve hundred of them were killed or made prisoners during the Revolution. They were to be found in the Army and Navy and behind the guns of privateers. There were twenty-five Nantucket whalemen in the crew of the *Ranger* when Paul Jones steered her across the Atlantic on that famous cruise which inspired the old forecastle song that begins:

> 'Tis of the gallant Yankee ship
> That flew the Stripes and Stars,
> And the whistling wind from the west nor'west
> Blew through her pitch pine spars.
> With her starboard tacks aboard, my boys,
> She hung upon the gale.
> On an autumn night we raised the light
> Off the Old Head of Kinsale.

Pitiful as was the situation of Nantucket, with its only industry wiped out and two hundred widows among the eight hundred families left on the island, the aftermath of war seemed almost as ruinous along the whole Atlantic coast. More ships could be built and there were thousands of adventurous sailors to man them, but where were the markets for the products of the farms and mills and plantations? The ports of Europe had been so long closed to American shipping that little demand was left for American goods. To the Government of England the people of the Republic were no longer fellow-countrymen but foreigners. As such they were subject to the Navigation Acts, and no cargoes could be sent to that kingdom unless in British vessels. The flourishing trade with the West Indies was made impossible for the same reason, a special Order in Council aiming at one fell stroke to "put an end to the building and increase of American vessels" and to finish the careers of three hundred West Indiamen already afloat. In the islands themselves the results were appalling. Fifteen thousand slaves died of starvation because the American traders were compelled to cease bringing them dried fish and corn during seasons in which their own crops were destroyed by hurricanes.

In 1776, one-third of the seagoing merchant marine of Great Britain had been bought or built to order in America because lumber was cheaper and wages were lower. This lucrative business was killed by a law which denied Englishmen the privilege of purchasing ships built in American yards.

So narrow and bitter was this commercial enmity, so ardent this desire to banish the Stars and Stripes from blue water, that Lord Sheffield in 1784 advised Parliament that the pirates of Algiers and Tripoli really benefited English commerce by preying on the shipping of weaker nations. "It is not probable that the American States will have a very free trade in the Mediterranean," said he. "It will not be to the interest of any of the great maritime Powers to protect them from the Barbary States. If they know their interests, they will not encourage the Americans to be carriers. That the Barbary States are advantageous to maritime Powers is certain."

Denied the normal ebb and flow of trade and commerce and with the imports from England far exceeding the value of the merchandise exported thence, the United States, already impoverished, was drained of its money, and a currency of dollars, guineas, joes, and moidores grew scarcer day by day. There was no help in a government which consisted of States united only in name. Congress comprised a handful of respectable gentlemen who had little power and less responsibility, quarreling among themselves for lack of better employment. Retaliation against England by means of legislation was utterly impossible. Each State looked after its commerce in its own peculiar fashion and the devil might take the hindmost. Their rivalries and jealousies were like those of petty kingdoms. If one State should close her ports to English ships, the others would welcome them in order to divert the trade, with no feeling of national pride or federal coöperation.

The Articles of Confederation had empowered Congress to make treaties of commerce, but only such as did not restrain the legislative power of any State from laying imposts and regulating exports and imports. If a foreign power imposed heavy duties upon American shipping, it was for the individual States and not for Congress to say whether the vessels of the offending nation should be allowed free entrance to the ports of the United States. It was folly to suppose, ran the common opinion, that if South Carolina should bar her ports to Spain because rice and indigo were excluded from the Spanish colonies, New Hampshire, which furnished masts and lumber for the Spanish Navy, ought to do the same. The idea of turning the whole matter over to Congress was considered preposterous by many intelligent Americans.

In these thirteen States were nearly three and a

quarter million people hemmed in a long and narrow strip between the sea and an unexplored wilderness in which the Indians were an ever present peril. The Southern States, including Maryland, prosperous agricultural regions, contained almost one-half the English-speaking population of America. As colonies, they had found the Old World eager for their rice, tobacco, indigo, and tar, and slavery was the means of labor so firmly established that one-fifth of the inhabitants were black. By contrast, the Northern States were still concerned with commerce as the very lifeblood of their existence. New England had not dreamed of the millions of spindles which should hum on the banks of her rivers and lure her young men and women from the farms to the clamorous factory towns. The city of New York had not yet outgrown its traffic in furs and its magnificent commercial destiny was still unrevealed. It was a considerable seaport but not yet a gateway. From Sandy Hook, however, to the stormy headlands of Maine, it was a matter of life and death that ships should freely come and go with cargoes to exchange. All other resources were trifling in comparison.

CHAPTER IV

IN such compelling circumstances as these, necessity became the mother of achievement. There is nothing finer in American history than the dogged fortitude and high-hearted endeavor with which the merchant seamen returned to their work after the Revolution and sought and found new markets for their wares. It was then that Salem played that conspicuous part which was, for a generation, to overshadow the activities of all other American seaports. Six thousand privateersmen had signed articles in her taverns, as many as the total population of the town, and they filled it with a spirit of enterprise and daring. Not for them the stupid monotony of voyages coastwise if more hazardous ventures beckoned and there were havens and islands unvexed by trade where bold men might win profit and perhaps fight for life and cargo.

Now there dwelt in Salem one of the great men

of his time, Elias Hasket Derby, the first American millionaire, and very much more than this. He was a shipping merchant with a vision and with the hard-headed sagacity to make his dreams come true. His was a notable seafaring family, to begin with. His father, Captain Richard Derby, born in 1712, had dispatched his small vessels to the West Indies and Virginia and with the returns from these voyages he had loaded assorted cargoes for Spain and Madeira and had the proceeds remitted in bills of exchange to London or in wine, salt, fruit, oil, lead, and handkerchiefs to America. Richard Derby's vessels had eluded or banged away at the privateers during the French War from 1756 to 1763, mounting from eight to twelve guns, "with four cannon below decks for close quarters." Of such a temper was this old sea-dog who led the militia and defiantly halted General Gage's regulars at the North River bridge in Salem, two full months before the skirmish at Lexington. Eight of the nineteen cannon which it was proposed to seize from the patriots had been taken from the ships of Captain Richard Derby and stored in his warehouse for the use of the Provincial Congress.

It was Richard's son, Captain John Derby, who

*ELIAS HASKET DERBY, MERCHANT AND SHIPBUILDER,
OF SALEM*

Painting by James Frothingham. In the Peabody Museum, Salem.
Massachusetts.

carried to England in the swift schooner *Quero* the
first news of the affair at Lexington, ahead of the
King's messenger. A sensational arrival, if ever
there was one! This Salem shipmaster, cracking
on sail like a proper son of his sire, making the
passage in twenty-nine days and handsomely
beating the lubberly Royal Express Packet *Sukey*
which left Boston four days sooner, and startling
the British nation with the tidings which meant
the loss of an American empire! A singular coin-
cidence was that this same Captain John Derby
should have been the first mariner to inform the
United States that peace had come, when he
arrived from France in 1783 with the message that
a treaty had been signed.

Elias Hasket Derby was another son of Richard.
When his manifold energies were crippled by the
war, he diverted his ability and abundant resources
into privateering. He was interested in at least
eighty of the privateers out of Salem, invariably
subscribing for such shares as might not be taken
up by his fellow-townsmen. He soon perceived
that many of these craft were wretchedly unfit for
the purpose and were easily captured or wrecked.
It was characteristic of his genius that he should
establish shipyards of his own, turn his attention

to naval architecture, and begin to build a class of vessels vastly superior in size, model, and speed to any previously launched in the colonies. They were designed to meet the small cruiser of the British Navy on even terms and were remarkably successful, both in enriching their owner and in defying the enemy.

At the end of the war Elias Hasket Derby discovered that these fine ships were too large and costly to ply up and down the coast. Instead of bewailing his hard lot, he resolved to send them to the other side of the globe. At a time when the British and the Dutch East India companies insolently claimed a monopoly of the trade of the Orient, when American merchant seamen had never ventured beyond the two Atlantics, this was a conception which made of commerce a surpassing romance and heralded the golden era of the nation's life upon the sea.

His *Grand Turk* of three hundred tons was promptly fitted out for a pioneering voyage as far as the Cape of Good Hope. Salem knew her as "the great ship" and yet her hull was not quite one hundred feet long. Safely Captain Jonathan Ingersoll took her out over the long road, his navigating equipment consisting of a few erroneous maps and charts, a sextant, and Guthrie's Geographical Grammar. In Table Bay he sold his cargo of provisions and then visited the coast of Guinea to dispose of his rum for ivory and gold-dust but brought not a single slave back, Mr. Derby having declared that "he would rather sink the whole capital employed than directly or indirectly be concerned in so infamous a trade" — an unusual point of view for a shipping merchant of New England in 1784!

Derby ships were first to go to Mauritius, then called the Isle of France, first at Calcutta, and among the earliest to swing at anchor off Canton. When Elias Hasket Derby decided to invade this rich East India commerce, he sent his eldest son, Elias Hasket, Jr., to England and the Continent after a course at Harvard. The young man became a linguist and made a thorough study of English and French methods of trade. Having laid this foundation for the venture, the son was now sent to India, where he lived for three years in the interests of his house, building up a trade almost fabulously profitable.

How fortunes were won in those stirring days may be discerned from the record of young Derby's ventures while in the Orient. In 1788 the proceeds of one cargo enabled him to buy a ship and a brigantine in the Isle of France. These two vessels he sent to Bombay to load with cotton. Two other ships of his fleet, the *Astrea* and *Light Horse*, were filled at Calcutta and Rangoon and ordered to Salem. It was found, when the profits of these transactions were reckoned, that the little squadron had earned $100,000 above all outlay.

To carry on such a business as this enlisted many men and industries. While the larger ships were making their distant voyages, the brigs and schooners were gathering cargoes for them, crossing to Gothenburg and St. Petersburg for iron, duck, and hemp, to France, Spain, and Madeira for wine and lead, to the French West Indies for molasses to be turned into rum, to New York, Philadelphia, and Richmond for flour, provisions, and tobacco. These shipments were assembled in the warehouses on Derby Wharf and paid for the teas, coffees, pepper, muslin, silks, and ivory which the ships from the Far East were fetching home. In fourteen years the Derby ships made one hundred and twenty-five voyages to Europe and far eastern ports and out of the thirty-five vessels engaged only one was lost at sea.

It was in 1785 when the *Grand Turk*, on a second

THE SHIP "GRAND TURK"

Painting by a Chinese artist at Canton, on a punch-bowl, 1786. In the Peabody Museum, Salem, Massachusetts. The *Grand Turk* opened the American trade with China at Canton in 1785, and with the Dutch at the Isle of France in 1787. She was built for E. H. Derby in 1781.

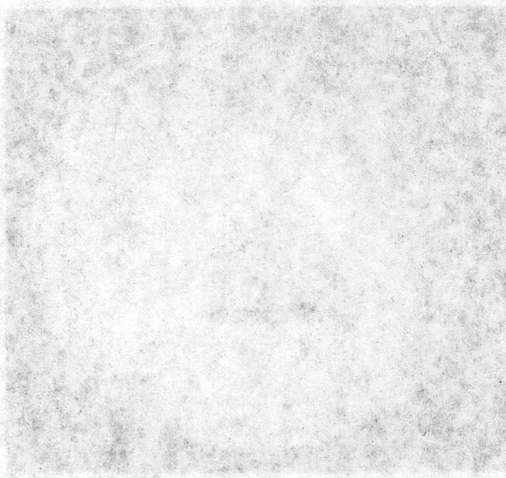

voyage, brought back a cargo of silks, teas, and nankeens from Batavia and China, that *The Independent Chronicle* of London, unconsciously humorous, was moved to affirm that "the Americans have given up all thought of a China trade which can never be carried on to advantage without some settlement in the East Indies."

As soon as these new sea-trails had been furrowed by the keels of Elias Hasket Derby, other Salem merchants were quick to follow in a rivalry which left no sea unexplored for virgin markets and which ransacked every nook and corner of barbarism which had a shore. Vessels slipped their cables and sailed away by night for some secret destination with whose savage potentate trade relations had been established. It might be Captain Jonathan Carnes who, while at the port of Bencoolen in 1793, heard that pepper grew wild on the northern coast of Sumatra. He whispered the word to the Salem owner, who sent him back in the schooner *Rajah* with only four guns and ten men. Eighteen months later, Jonathan Carnes returned to Salem with a cargo of pepper in bulk, the first direct importation, and cleared seven hundred per cent on the voyage. When he made ready to go again, keeping his business strictly to himself, other owners tracked him clear to Bencoolen, but there he vanished in the *Rajah*, and his secret with him, until he reappeared with another precious cargo of pepper. When, at length, he shared this trade with other vessels, it meant that Salem controlled the pepper market of Sumatra and for many years supplied a large part of the world's demand.

And so it happened that in the spicy warehouses that overlooked Salem Harbor there came to be stored hemp from Luzon, gum copal from Zanzibar, palm oil from Africa, coffee from Arabia, tallow from Madagascar, whale oil from the Antarctic, hides and wool from the Rio de la Plata, nutmeg and cloves from Malaysia. Such merchandise had been bought or bartered for by shipmasters who were much more than mere navigators. They had to be shrewd merchants on their own accounts, for the success or failure of a voyage was mostly in their hands. Carefully trained and highly intelligent men, they attained command in the early twenties and were able to retire, after a few years more afloat, to own ships and exchange the quarterdeck for the counting-room, and the cabin for the solid mansion and lawn on Derby Street. Every opportunity, indeed, was offered them to advance

their own fortunes. They sailed not for wages but
for handsome commissions and privileges — in
the Derby ships, five per cent of a cargo outward
bound, two and a half per cent of the freightage
home, five per cent profit on goods bought and
sold between foreign ports, and five per cent of
the cargo space for their own use.

Such was the system which persuaded the pick
and flower of young American manhood to choose
the sea as the most advantageous career possible.
There was the Crowninshield family, for example,
with five brothers all in command of ships before
they were old enough to vote and at one time all
five away from Salem, each in his own vessel and
three of them in the East India trade. "When
little boys," to quote from the memoirs of Benjamin Crowninshield, "they were all sent to a
common school and about their eleventh year
began their first particular study which should
develop them as sailors and ship captains. These
boys studied their navigation as little chaps of
twelve years old and were required to thoroughly
master the subject before being sent to sea. . . .
As soon as the art of navigation was mastered,
the youngsters were sent to sea, sometimes as
common sailors but commonly as ship's clerks, in

which position they were able to learn everything about the management of a ship without actually being a common sailor."

This was the practice in families of solid station and social rank, for to be a shipmaster was to follow the profession of a gentleman. Yet the bright lad who entered by way of the forecastle also played for high stakes. Soon promoted to the berth of mate, he was granted cargo space for his own adventures in merchandise and a share of the profits. In these days the youth of twenty-one is likely to be a college undergraduate, rated too callow and unfit to be intrusted with the smallest business responsibilities and tolerantly regarded as unable to take care of himself. It provokes both a smile and a glow of pride, therefore, to recall those seasoned striplings and what they did.

No unusual instance was that of Nathaniel Silsbee, later United States Senator from Massachusetts, who took command of the new ship *Benjamin* in the year 1792, laden with a costly cargo from Salem for the Cape of Good Hope and India, "with such instructions," says he, "as left the management of the voyage very much to my own discretion. Neither myself nor the chief mate, Mr. Charles Derby, had attained the age of

NATHANIEL SILSBEE

Painting by A. Hartwell, after Chester Harding. In the Peabody
Museum, Salem, Massachusetts.

JOSEPH PEABODY

Painting by Charles Osgood. In the Peabody Museum, Salem,
Massachusetts.

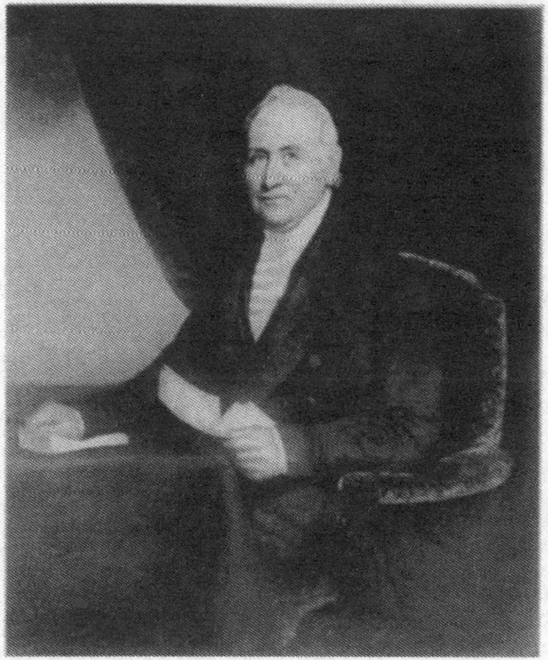

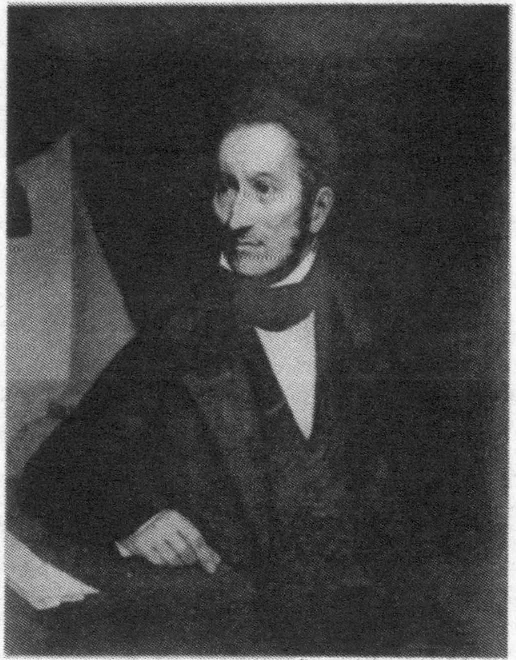

twenty-one years when we left home. I was not then twenty." This reminded him to speak of his own family. Of the three Silsbee brothers, "each of us obtained the command of vessels and the consignment of their cargoes before attaining the age of twenty years, viz., myself at the age of eighteen and a half, my brother William at nineteen and a half, and my brother Zachariah before he was twenty years old. Each and all of us left off going to sea before reaching the age of twenty-nine years."

How resourcefully these children of the sea could handle affairs was shown in this voyage of the *Benjamin*. While in the Indian Ocean young Silsbee fell in with a frigate which gave him news of the beginning of war between England and France. He shifted his course for Mauritius and there sold the cargo for a dazzling price in paper dollars, which he turned into Spanish silver. An embargo detained him for six months, during which this currency increased to three times the value of the paper money. He gave up the voyage to Calcutta, sold the Spanish dollars and loaded with coffee and spices for Salem. At the Cape of Good Hope, however, he discovered that he could earn a pretty penny by sending his cargo home in other ships and loading the *Benjamin* again for Mauritius. When, at length, he arrived in Salem harbor, after nineteen months away, his enterprises had reaped a hundred per cent for Elias Hasket Derby and his own share was the snug little fortune of four thousand dollars. Part of this he, of course, invested at sea, and at twenty-two he was part owner of the *Betsy*, East Indiaman, and on the road to independence.

As second mate in the *Benjamin* had sailed Richard Cleveland, another matured mariner of nineteen, who crowded into one life an Odyssey of adventure noteworthy even in that era and who had the knack of writing about it with rare skill and spirit. In 1797, when twenty-three years old, he was master of the bark *Enterprise* bound from Salem to Mocha for coffee. The voyage was abandoned at Havre and he sent the mate home with the ship, deciding to remain abroad and gamble for himself with the chances of the sea. In France he bought on credit a "cutter-sloop" of forty-three tons, no larger than the yachts whose owners think it venturesome to take them off soundings in summer cruises. In this little box of a craft he planned to carry a cargo of merchandise to the Cape of Good Hope and thence to Mauritius.

His crew included two men, a black cook, and a brace of boys who were hastily shipped at Havre. "Fortunately they were all so much in debt as not to want any time to spend their advance, but were ready at the instant, and with this motley crew, (who, for aught I knew, were robbers or pirates) I put to sea." The only sailor of the lot was a Nantucket lad who was made mate and had to be taught the rudiments of navigation while at sea. Of the others he had this to say, in his light-hearted manner:

The first of my fore-mast hands is a great, surly, crabbed, raw-boned, ignorant Prussian who is so timid aloft that the mate has frequently been obliged to do his duty there. I believe him to be more of a soldier than a sailor, though he has often assured me that he has been a boatswain's mate of a Dutch Indiaman, which I do not believe as he hardly knows how to put two ends of a rope together. . . . My cook . . . a good-natured negro and a tolerable cook, so unused to a vessel that in the smoothest weather he cannot walk fore and aft without holding onto something with both hands. This fear proceeds from the fact that he is so tall and slim that if he should get a cant it might be fatal to him. I did not think America could furnish such a specimen of the negro race . . . nor did I ever see such a simpleton. It is impossible to teach him anything and . . . he can hardly tell the main-halliards from the mainstay.

Next is an English boy of seventeen years old, who

from having lately had the small-pox is feeble and almost blind, a miserable object, but pity for his misfortunes induces me to make his duty as easy as possible. Finally I have a little ugly French boy, the very image of a baboon, who from having served for some time on different privateers has all the tricks of a veteran man-of-war's man, though only thirteen years old, and by having been in an English prison, has learned enough of the language to be a proficient in swearing.

With these human scrapings for a ship's company, the cutter *Caroline* was three months on her solitary way as far as the Cape of Good Hope, where the inhabitants "could not disguise their astonishment at the size of the vessel, the boyish appearance of the master and mate, and the queer and unique characters of the two men and boy who composed the crew." The English officials thought it strange indeed, suspecting some scheme of French spies or smuggled dispatches, but Richard Cleveland's petition to the Governor, Lord McCartney, ingenuously patterned after certain letters addressed to noblemen as found in an old magazine aboard his vessel, won the day for him and he was permitted to sell the cutter and her cargo, having changed his mind about proceeding farther.

Taking passage to Batavia, he looked about for another venture but found nothing to his liking and wandered on to Canton, where he was attracted by the prospect of a voyage to the northwest coast of America to buy furs from the Indians. In a cutter no larger than the *Caroline* he risked all his cash and credit, stocking her with $20,000 worth of assorted merchandise for barter, and put out across the Pacific, "having on board twenty-one persons, consisting, except two Americans, of English, Irish, Swedes and French, but principally the first, who were runaways from the men-of-war and Indiamen, and two from a Botany Bay ship who had made their escape, for we were obliged to take such as we could get, served to complete a list of as accomplished villains as ever disgraced any country."

After a month of weary, drenching hardship off the China coast, this crew of cutthroats mutinied. With a loyal handful, including the black cook, Cleveland locked up the provisions, mounted two four-pounders on the quarter-deck, rammed them full of grape-shot, and fetched up the flint-lock muskets and pistols from the cabin. The mutineers were then informed that if they poked their heads above the hatches he would blow them overboard. Losing enthusiasm and weakened by hunger, they asked to be set ashore; so the skipper marooned the lot. For two days the cutter lay off-shore while a truce was argued, the upshot being that four of the rascals gave in and the others were left behind.

Fifty days more of it and, washed by icy seas, racked and storm-beaten, the vessel made Nor-folk Sound. So small was the crew, so imminent the danger that the Indians might take her by boarding, that screens of hides were rigged along the bulwarks to hide the deck from view. Stranded and getting clear, warding off attacks, Captain Richard Cleveland stayed two months on the wilderness coast of Oregon, trading one musket for eight prime sea-otter skins until there was no more room below. Sixty thousand dollars was the value of the venture when he sailed for China by way of the Sandwich Islands, forty thousand of profit, and he was twenty-five years old with the zest for roving undiminished.

He next appeared in Calcutta, buying a twenty-five-ton pilot boat under the Danish flag for a fling at Mauritius and a speculation in prizes brought in by French privateers. Finding none in port, he loaded seven thousand bags of coffee in a ship for Copenhagen and conveyed as a passenger a kindred spirit, young Nathaniel Shaler, whom he took into partnership. At Hamburg these two bought a fast brig, the *Lelia Byrd*, to try their fortune on the west coast of South America, and recruited a third partner, a boyish Polish nobleman, Count de Rousillon, who had been an aide to Kosciusko. Three seafaring musketeers, true gentlemen rovers, all under thirty, sailing out to beard the viceroys of Spain!

From Valparaiso, where other American ships were detained and robbed, they adroitly escaped and steered north to Mexico and California. At San Diego they fought their way out of the harbor, silencing the Spanish fort with their six guns. Then to Canton with furs, and Richard Cleveland went home at thirty years of age after seven years' absence and voyaging twice around the world, having wrested success from almost every imaginable danger and obstacle, with $70,000 to make him a rich man in his own town. He was neither more nor less than an American sailor of the kind that made the old merchant marine magnificent.

It was true romance, also, when the first American shipmasters set foot in mysterious Japan, a half century before Perry's squadron shattered the immemorial isolation of the land of the Shoguns and the Samurai. Only the Dutch had been

permitted to hold any foreign intercourse whatever
with this hermit nation and for two centuries they
had maintained their singular commercial monopoly at a price measured in terms of the deep-
est degradation of dignity and respect. The few
Dutch merchants suffered to reside in Japan were
restricted to a small island in Nagasaki harbor,
leaving it only once in four years when the Resi-
dent, or chief agent, journeyed to Yeddo to offer
gifts and most humble obeisance to the Shogun,
"creeping forward on his hands and feet, and falling
on his knees, bowed his head to the ground, and
retired again in absolute silence, crawling exactly
like a crab," said one of these pilgrims who added:
"We may not keep Sundays or fast days, or allow
our spiritual hymns or prayers to be heard; never
mention the name of Christ. Besides these things,
we have to submit to other insulting imputations
which are always painful to a noble heart. The
reason which impels the Dutch to bear all these
sufferings so patiently is simply the love of gain."

In return for these humiliations the Dutch East
India Company was permitted to send one or two
ships a year from Batavia to Japan and to export
copper, silk, gold, camphor, porcelain, bronze, and
rare woods. The American ship *Franklin* arrived

at Batavia in 1799 and Captain James Devereux of Salem learned that a charter was offered for one of these annual voyages. After a deal of Yankee dickering with the hard-headed Dutchmen, a bargain was struck and the *Franklin* sailed for Nagasaki with cloves, chintz, sugar, tin, black pepper, sapan wood, and elephants' teeth. The instructions were elaborate and punctilious, salutes to be fired right and left, nine guns for the Emperor's guard while passing in, thirteen guns at the anchorage; all books on board to be sealed up in a cask, Bibles in particular, and turned over to the Japanese officials, all firearms sent ashore, ship dressed with colors whenever the "Commissaries of the Chief" graciously came aboard, and a carpet on deck for them to sit upon.

Two years later, the *Margaret* of Salem made the same sort of a voyage, and in both instances the supercargoes, one of whom happened to be a younger brother of Captain Richard Cleveland, wrote journals of the extraordinary episode. For these mariners alone was the curtain lifted which concealed the feudal Japan from the eyes of the civilized world. Alert and curious, these Yankee traders explored the narrow streets of Nagasaki, visited temples, were handsomely entertained by officers and merchants, and exchanged their wares in the market-place. They were as much at home, no doubt, as when buying piculs of pepper from a rajah of Qualah Battoo, or dining with an elderly mandarin of Cochin China. It was not too much to say that "the profuse stores of knowledge brought by every ship's crew, together with unheard of curiosities from every savage shore, gave the community of Salem a rare alertness of intellect."

It was a Salem bark, the *Lydia*, that first displayed the American flag to the natives of Guam in 1801. She was chartered by the Spanish government of Manila to carry to the Marianne Islands, as those dots on the chart of the Pacific were then called, the new Governor, his family, his suite, and his luggage. First Mate William Haswell kept a diary in a most conscientious fashion, and here and there one gleans an item with a humor of its own. "Now having to pass through dangerous straits," he observes, "we went to work to make boarding nettings and to get our arms in the best order, but had we been attacked we should have been taken with ease. Between Panay and Negros all the passengers were in the greatest confusion for fear of being taken and put to death in the dark and not have time to say their prayers."

The decks were in confusion most of the time, what with the Governor, his lady, three children, two servant girls and twelve men servants, a friar and his servant, a judge and two servants, not to mention some small hogs, two sheep, an ox, and a goat to feed the passengers who were too dainty for sea provender. The friar was an interesting character. A great pity that the worthy mate of the *Lydia* should not have been more explicit! It intrigues the reader of his manuscript diary to be told that "the Friar was praying night and day but it would not bring a fair wind. His behavior was so bad that we were forced to send him to Coventry, or in other words, no one would speak to him."

The Spanish governors of Guam had in operation an economic system which compelled the admiration of this thrifty Yankee mate. The natives wore very few clothes, he concluded, because the Governor was the only shopkeeper and he insisted on a profit of at least eight hundred per cent. There was a native militia regiment of a thousand men who were paid ten dollars a year. With this cash they bought Bengal goods, cottons, Chinese pans, pots, knives, and hoes at the Governor's store, so that "all this money never left the

Governor's hands. It was fetched to him by the galleons in passing, and when he was relieved he carried it with him to Manila, often to the amount of eighty or ninety thousand dollars." A glimpse of high finance without a flaw!

There is pathos, simple and moving, in the stories of shipwreck and stranding on hostile or desert coasts. These disasters were far more frequent then than now, because navigation was partly guesswork and ships were very small. Among these tragedies was that of the *Commerce*, bound from Boston to Bombay in 1793. The captain lost his bearings and thought he was off Malabar when the ship piled up on the beach in the night. The nearest port was Muscat and the crew took to the boats in the hope of reaching it. Stormy weather drove them ashore where armed Arabs on camels stripped them of clothes and stores and left them to die among the sand dunes.

On foot they trudged day after day in the direction of Muscat, and how they suffered and what they endured was told by one of the survivors, young Daniel Saunders. Soon they began to drop out and die in their tracks in the manner of "Benjamin Williams, William Leghorn, and Thomas Barnard whose bodies were exposed naked to the scorching sun and finding their strength and spirits quite exhausted they lay down expecting nothing but death for relief." The next to be left behind was Mr. Robert Williams, merchant and part owner, "and we therefore with reluctance abandoned him to the mercy of God, suffering ourselves all the horrors that fill the mind at the approach of death." Near the beach and a forlorn little oasis, they stumbled across Charles Lapham, who had become separated from them. He had been without water for five days "and after many efforts he got upon his feet and endeavored to walk. Seeing him in so wretched a condition I could not but sympathize enough with him in his torments to go back with him" toward water two miles away, "which both my other companions refused to do. Accordingly they walked forward while I went back a considerable distance with Lapham until, his strength failing him, he suddenly fell on the ground, nor was he able to rise again or even speak to me. Finding it vain to stay with him, I covered him with sprays and leaves which I tore from an adjacent tree, it being the last friendly office I could do him."

Eight living skeletons left of eighteen strong

seamen tottered into Muscat and were cared for
by the English consul. Daniel Saunders worked
his passage to England, was picked up by a press-
gang, escaped, and so returned to Salem. It was
the fate of Juba Hill, the black cook from Boston, to be detained among the Arabs as a slave.
It is worth noting that a black sea-cook figured in
many of these tales of daring and disaster, and
among them was the heroic and amazing figure of
one Peter Jackson who belonged in the brig *Ceres*.
While running down the river from Calcutta she
was thrown on her beam ends and Peter, perhaps
dumping garbage over the rail, took a header.
Among the things tossed to him as he floated away
was a sail-boom on which he was swiftly carried
out of sight by the turbid current. All on board
concluded that Peter Jackson had been eaten by
sharks or crocodiles and it was so reported when
they arrived home. An administrator was appointed for his goods and chattels and he was
officially deceased in the eyes of the law. A year
or so later this unconquerable sea-cook appeared
in the streets of Salem, grinning a welcome to former shipmates who fled from him in terror as a
ghostly visitation. He had floated twelve hours
on his sail-boom, it seemed, fighting off the sharks

with his feet, and finally drifting ashore. "He had hard work to do away with the impressions of being dead," runs the old account, "but succeeded and was allowed the rights and privileges of the living."

The community of interests in these voyages of long ago included not only the ship's company but also the townspeople, even the boys and girls, who entrusted their little private speculations or "adventures" to the captain. It was a custom which flourished well into the nineteenth century. These memoranda are sprinkled through the account books of the East Indiamen out of Salem and Boston. It might be Miss Harriet Elkins who requested the master of the *Messenger* "please to purchase at Calcutta two net beads with draperies; if at Batavia or any spice market, nutmegs or mace; or if at Canton, two Canton shawls of the enclosed colors at $5 per shawl. Enclosed is $10."

Again, it might be Mr. John R. Tucker who ventured in the same ship one hundred Spanish dollars to be invested in coffee and sugar, or Captain Nathaniel West who risked in the *Astrea* fifteen boxes of spermaceti candles and a pipe of Teneriffe wine. It is interesting to discover what was done with Mr. Tucker's hundred Spanish dollars, as invested for him by the skipper of the *Messenger* at Batavia and duly accounted for. Ten bags of coffee were bought for $83.30, the extra expenses of duty, boat-hire, and sacking bringing the total outlay to $90.19. The coffee was sold at Antwerp on the way home for $183.75, and Mr. Tucker's handsome profit on the adventure was therefore $93.56, or more than one hundred per cent.

It was all a grand adventure, in fact, and the word was aptly chosen to fit this ocean trade. The merchant freighted his ship and sent her out to vanish from his ken for months and months of waiting, with the greater part of his savings, perhaps, in goods and specie beneath her hatches. No cable messages kept him in touch with her nor were there frequent letters from the master. Not until her signal was displayed by the fluttering flags of the headland station at the harbor mouth could he know whether he had gained or lost a fortune. The spirit of such merchants was admirably typified in the last venture of Elias Hasket Derby in 1798, when unofficial war existed between the United States and France.

THE SHIP "MOUNT VERNON," ESCAPING FROM THE
FRENCH FLEET, 1799

Painting by M. Corné. 1799. In the Peabody Museum, Salem,
Massachusetts.

American ships were everywhere seeking refuge
from the privateers under the tricolor, which fairly
ran amuck in the routes of trade. For this reason
it meant a rich reward to land a cargo abroad. The
ship *Mount Vernon*, commanded by Captain Elias
Hasket Derby, Jr., was laden with sugar and coffee
for Mediterranean ports, and was prepared for trouble, with twenty guns mounted and fifty men to
handle them. A smart ship and a powerful one, she
raced across to Cape Saint Vincent in sixteen days,
which was clipper speed. She ran into a French fleet
of sixty sail, exchanged broadsides with the nearest,
and showed her stern to the others.

We arrived at 12 o'clock [wrote Captain Derby from
Gibraltar] popping at Frenchmen all the forenoon. At
10 A.M. off Algeciras Point we were seriously attacked
by a large latineer who had on board more than one
hundred men. He came so near our broadside as to
allow our six-pound grape to do execution handsomely.
We then bore away and gave him our stern guns in a
cool and deliberate manner, doing apparently great execution. Our bars having cut his sails considerably,
he was thrown into confusion, struck both his ensign
and his pennant. I was then puzzled to know what to
do with so many men; our ship was running large with
all her steering sails out, so that we could not immediately bring her to the wind, and we were directly off
Algeciras Point from whence I had reason to fear she

might receive assistance, and my port Gibraltar in
full view. These were circumstances that induced me
to give up the gratification of bringing him in. It was,
however, a satisfaction to flog the rascal in full view of
the English fleet who were to leeward.

CHAPTER V

YANKEE VIKINGS AND NEW TRADE ROUTES

Soon after the Revolution the spirit of commercial exploration began to stir in other ports than Salem. Out from New York sailed the ship *Empress of China* in 1784 for the first direct voyage to Canton, to make the acquaintance of a vast nation absolutely unknown to the people of the United States, nor had one in a million of the industrious and highly civilized Chinese ever so much as heard the name of the little community of barbarians who dwelt on the western shore of the North Atlantic. The oriental dignitaries in their silken robes graciously welcomed the foreign ship with the strange flag and showed a lively interest in the map spread upon the cabin table, offering every facility to promote this new market for their silks and teas. After an absence of fifteen months the *Empress of China* returned to her home port and her pilgrimage aroused so much attention that the report of the supercargo, Samuel Shaw, was read in Congress.

Surpassing this achievement was that of Captain Stewart Dean, who very shortly afterward had his fling at the China trade in an eighty-ton sloop built at Albany. He was a stout-hearted old privateersman of the Revolution whom nothing could dismay, and in this tiny *Experiment* of his he won merited fame as one of the American pioneers of blue water. Fifteen men and boys sailed with him, drilled and disciplined as if the sloop were a frigate, and when the *Experiment* hauled into the stream, off Battery Park, New York, "martial music and the boatswain's whistle were heard on board with all the pomp and circumstance of war." Typhoons and Malay proas, Chinese pirates and unknown shoals, had no terrors for Stewart Dean. He saw Canton for himself, found a cargo, and drove home again in a four months' passage, which was better than many a clipper could do at a much later day. Smallest and bravest of the first Yankee East Indiamen, this taut sloop, with the boatswain's pipe trilling cheerily and all hands ready with cutlases and pikes to repel boarders, was by no means the least important vessel that ever passed in by Sandy Hook.

In the beginnings of this picturesque relation
with the Far East, Boston lagged behind Salem,
but her merchants, too, awoke to the opportunity
and so successfully that for generations there were
no more conspicuous names and shipping-houses
in the China trade than those of Russell, Perkins,
and Forbes. The first attempt was very ambitious
and rather luckless. The largest merchantman
ever built at that time in the United States was
launched at Quincy in 1789 to rival the towering
ships of the British East India Company. This
Massachusetts created a sensation. Her departure
was a national event. She embodied the dreams of
a Captain Randall and of the Samuel Shaw who
had gone as supercargo in the *Empress of China*.
They formed a partnership and were able to find
the necessary capital.

This six-hundred-ton ship loomed huge in the
eyes of the crowds which visited her. She was
in fact no larger than such four-masted coasting
schooners as claw around Hatteras with deck-loads
of Georgia pine or fill with coal for down East, and
manage it comfortably with seven or eight men
for a crew. The *Massachusetts*, however, sailed in
all the old-fashioned state and dignity of a master,
four mates, a purser, surgeon, carpenter, gunner,

6

four quartermasters, three midshipmen, a cooper, two cooks, a steward, and fifty seamen. The second officer was Amasa Delano, a man even more remarkable than the ship, who wandered far and wide and wrote a fascinating book about his voyages, a classic of its kind, — the memoirs of an American merchant mariner of a breed long since extinct.

While the *Massachusetts* was fitting out at Boston, one small annoyance ruffled the auspicious undertaking. Three different crews were signed before a full complement could be persuaded to tarry in the forecastle. The trouble was caused by a fortune-teller of Lynn, Moll Pitcher by name, who predicted disaster for the ship. Now every honest sailor knows that certain superstitions are gospel fact, such as the bad luck brought by a cross-eyed Finn, a black cat, or going to sea on Friday, and these eighteenth century shellbacks must not be too severely chided for deserting while they had the chance. As it turned out, the voyage did have a sorry ending and death overtook an astonishingly large number of the ship's people.

Though she had been designed and built by master craftsmen of New England who knew their

trade surpassingly well, it was discovered when
the ship arrived at Canton that her timbers were
already rotting. They were of white oak which
had been put into her green instead of properly
seasoned. This blunder wrecked the hopes of her
owners. To cap it, the cargo of masts and spars
had also been stowed while wet and covered with
mud and ice, and the hatches had been battened.
As a result the air became so foul with decay that
several hundred barrels of beef were spoiled. To
repair the ship was beyond the means of Captain
Randall and Samuel Shaw, and reluctantly they
sold her to the Danish East India Company at
a heavy loss. Nothing could have been more
unexpected than to find that, for once, the expe-
rienced shipbuilders had been guilty of a mis-
calculation.

The crew scattered, and perhaps the prediction
of the fortune-teller of Lynn followed their roving
courses, for when Captain Amasa Delano tried to
trace them a few years later, he jotted down such
obituaries as these on the list of names:

John Harris. A slave in Algiers at last accounts.
Roger Dyer. Died and thrown overboard off Cape
Horn.
William Williams. Lost overboard off Japan.

James Crowley. Murdered by the Chinese near Macao.

John Johnson. Died on board an English Indiaman.

Seth Stowell. Was drowned at Whampoa in 1790.

Jeremiah Chace. Died with the small-pox at Whampoa in 1791.

Humphrey Chadburn. Shot and died at Whampoa in 1791.

Samuel Tripe. Drowned off Java Head in 1790.

James Stackpole. Murdered by the Chinese.

Nicholas Nicholson. Died with the leprosy at Macao.

William Murphy. Killed by Chinese pirates.

Larry Conner. Killed at sea.

There were more of these gruesome items — so many of them that it appears as though no more than a handful of this stalwart crew survived the *Massachusetts* by a dozen years. Incredible as it sounds, Captain Delano's roster accounted for fifty of them as dead while he was still in the prime of life, and most of them had been snuffed out by violence. As for his own career, it was overcast by no such unlucky star, and he passed unscathed through all the hazards and vicissitudes that could be encountered in that rugged and heroic era of endeavor. Set adrift in Canton when the *Massachusetts* was sold, he promptly turned his hand to

repairing a large Danish ship which had been
wrecked by storm, and he virtually rebuilt her to
the great satisfaction of the owners.

Thence, with money in his pocket, young Delano went to Macao, where he fell in with Commodore John McClure of the English Navy, who was
in command of an expedition setting out to explore
a part of the South Seas, including the Pelew
Islands, New Guinea, New Holland, and the Spice
Islands. The Englishman liked this resourceful
Yankee seaman and did him the honor to say,
recalls Delano, "that he considered I should be a
very useful man to him as a seaman, an officer, or a
ship-builder; and if it was agreeable to me to go on
board the *Panther* with him, I should receive the
same pay and emoluments with his lieutenants and
astronomers." A signal honor it was at a time
when no love was lost between British and American seafarers who had so recently fought each
other afloat.

And so Amasa Delano embarked as a lieutenant of
the Bombay Marine, to explore tropic harbors and
lagoons until then unmapped and to parley with
dusky kings. Commodore McClure, diplomatic
and humane, had almost no trouble with the un-
tutored islanders, except on the coast of New

Guinea, where the *Panther* was attacked by a
swarm of canoes and the surgeon was killed. It
was a spirited little affair, four-foot arrows pelting
like hail across the deck, a cannon hurling grape-
shot from the taffrail, Amasa Delano hit in the
chest and pulling out the arrow to jump to his duty
again.

Only a few years earlier the mutineers of the
Bounty had established themselves on Pitcairn
Island, and Delano was able to compile the first
complete narrative of this extraordinary colony,
which governed itself in the light of the primitive
Christian virtues. There was profound wisdom
in the comment of Amasa Delano: "While the
present natural, simple, and affectionate character
prevails among these descendants of the mutineers,
they will be delightful to our minds, they will be
amiable and acceptable in the sight of God, and
they will be useful and happy among themselves.
Let it be our fervent prayer that neither canting
and hypocritical emissaries from schools of artifi-
cial theology on the one hand, nor sensual and
licentious crews and adventurers on the other,
may ever enter the charming village of Pitcairn
to give disease to the minds or the bodies of the
unsuspecting inhabitants."

Two years of this intensely romantic existence, and Delano started homeward. But there was a chance of profit at Mauritius, and there he bought a tremendous East Indiaman of fourteen hundred tons as a joint venture with a Captain Stewart and put a crew of a hundred and fifty men on board. She had been brought in by a French privateer and Delano was moved to remark, with an indignation which was much in advance of his times: "Privateering is entirely at variance with the first principle of honorable warfare. . . . This system of licensed robbery enables a wicked and mercenary man to insult and injure even neutral friends on the ocean; and when he meets an honest sailor who may have all his earnings on board his ship but who carries an enemy's flag, he plunders him of every cent and leaves him the poor consolation that it is done according to law. . . . When the Malay subjects of Abba Thule cut down the cocoanut trees of an enemy, in the spirit of private revenge, he asked them why they acted in opposition to the principles on which they knew he always made and conducted a war. They answered, and let the reason make us humble, 'The English do so.'"

In his grand East Indiaman young Captain

Delano traded on the coast of India but soon came to grief. The enterprise had been too large for him to swing with what cash and credit he could muster, and the ship was sold from under him to pay her debts. Again on the beach, with one solitary gold moidore in his purse, he found a friendly American skipper who offered him a passage to Philadelphia, which he accepted with the pious reflection that, although his mind was wounded and mortified by the financial disaster, his motives had been perfectly pure and honest. He never saw his native land with so little pleasure as on this return to it, he assures us, and the shore on which he would have leaped with delight was covered with gloom and sadness.

Now what makes it so well worth while to sketch in brief outline the careers of one and another of these bygone shipmasters is that they accurately reflected the genius and the temper of their generation. There was, in truth, no such word as failure in their lexicon. It is this quality that appeals to us beyond all else. Thrown on their beam ends, they were presently planning something else, eager to shake dice with destiny and with courage unbroken. It was so with Amasa Delano, who promptly went to work "with what spirits I

could revive within me. After a time they returned to their former elasticity."

He obtained a position as master builder in a
shipyard, saved some money, borrowed more, and
with one of his brothers was soon blithely building
a vessel of two hundred tons for a voyage into the
Pacific and to the northwest coast after seals.
They sailed along Patagonia and found much
to interest them, dodged in and out of the ports
of Chili and Peru, and incidentally recaptured a
Spanish ship which was in the hands of the slaves
who formed her cargo.

This was all in the day's work and happened
at the island of Santa Maria, not far from Juan
Fernandez, where Captain Delano's *Perseverance*
found the high-pooped *Tryal* in a desperate state.
Spanish sailors who had survived the massacre
were leaping overboard or scrambling up to the
mastheads while the African savages capered
on deck and flourished their weapons. Captain
Delano liked neither the Spaniard nor the slave-
trade, but it was his duty to help fellow seamen in
distress; so he cleared for action and ordered two
boats away to attend to the matter. The chief
mate, Rufus Low, was in charge, and a gallant
sailor he showed himself. They had to climb the

high sides of the *Tryal* and carry, in hand-to-hand conflict, the barricades of water-casks and bales of matting which the slaves had built across the deck. There was no hanging back, and even a mite of a midshipman from Boston pranced into it with his dirk. The negroes were well armed and fought ferociously. The mate was seriously wounded, four seamen were stabbed, the Spanish first mate had two musket balls in him, and a passenger was killed in the fray.

Having driven the slaves below and battened them down, the American party returned next morning to put the irons on them. A horrid sight confronted them. Thirsting for vengeance, the Spanish sailors had spread-eagled several of the negroes to ringbolts in the deck and were shaving the living flesh from them with razor-edged boarding lances. Captain Delano thereupon disarmed these brutes and locked them up in their turn, taking possession of the ship until he could restore order. The sequel was that he received the august thanks of the Viceroy of Chili and a gold medal from His Catholic Majesty. As was the custom, the guilty slaves, poor wretches, were condemned to be dragged to the gibbet at the tails of mules, to be hanged, their bodies burned, and their heads stuck upon poles in the plaza.

It was while in this Chilean port of Talcahuano that Amasa Delano heard the tale of the British whaler which had sailed just before his arrival. He tells it so well that I am tempted to quote it as a generous tribute to a sailor of a rival race. After all, they were sprung from a common stock and blood was thicker than water. Besides, it is the sort of yarn that ought to be dragged to the light of day from its musty burial between the covers of Delano's rare and ancient *Voyages and Travels*.

The whaler *Betsy*, it seems, went in and anchored under the guns of the forts to seek provisions and make repairs. The captain went ashore to interview the officials, leaving word that no Spaniards should be allowed to come aboard because of the bad feeling against the English. Three or four large boats filled with troops presently veered alongside and were ordered to keep clear. This command was resented, and the troops opened fire, followed by the forts. Now for the deed of a man with his two feet under him.

The chief officer of the *Betsy* whose name was Hudson, a man of extraordinary bravery, cut his cable and his ship swung the wrong way, with her head in shore, passing close to several Spanish ships which, with every vessel in the harbor that could bring a gun to bear, together with three hundred soldiers in boats and on ship's decks and the two batteries, all kept up a constant fire on him. The wind was light, nearly a calm. The shot flew so thick that it was difficult for him to make sail, some part of the rigging being cut away every minute.

He kept his men at the guns, and when the ship swung her broadside so as to bear upon any of the Spanish ships, he kept up a fire at them. In this situation the brave fellow continued to lie for three-quarters of an hour before he got his topsails sheeted home. The action continued in this manner for near an hour and a half. He succeeded in getting the ship to sea, however, in defiance of all the force that could be brought against him. The ship was very much cut to pieces in sails, rigging, and hull; and a considerable number of men were killed and wounded on board.

Hudson kept flying from one part of the deck to the other during the whole time of action, encouraging and threatening the men as occasion required. He kept a musket in his hand most part of the time, firing when he could find the leisure. Some of the men came aft and begged him to give up the ship, telling him they should all be killed — that the carpenter had all one side of him shot away — that one man was cut in halves with a double-headed shot as he was going aloft to loose the foretopsail and the body had fallen on deck in two separate parts — that such a man was killed at his duty on the forecastle, and one more had been killed in the maintop — that Sam, Jim, Jack, and Tom were wounded — and that they would do nothing more towards getting the ship out of the harbor.

His reply to them was, "then you shall be sure to die, for if they do not kill you I will, so sure as you persist in any such cowardly resolution," saying at the same time, "*Out she goes, or down she goes.*"

By this resolute and determined conduct he kept the men to their duty and succeeded in accomplishing one of the most daring enterprises perhaps ever attempted.

An immortal phrase, this simple dictum of first mate Hudson of the *Betsy*, "Out she goes, or down she goes," and not unworthy of being mentioned in the same breath with Farragut's "Damn the torpedoes."

Joined by his brother Samuel in the schooner *Pilgrim*, which was used as a tender in the sealing trade, Amasa Delano frequented unfamiliar beaches until he had taken his toll of skins and was ready to bear away for Canton to sell them. There were many Yankee ships after seals in those early days, enduring more peril and privation than the whalemen, roving over the South Pacific among the rock-bound islands unknown to the merchant navigator. The men sailed wholly on shares, a seaman receiving one per cent of the catch and the captain ten per cent, and they slaughtered the seal by the million, driving them from the most favored haunts within a few years. For instance, American ships first visited Mas a Fuera in 1797,

and Captain Delano estimated that during the seven
years following three million skins were taken to
China from this island alone. He found as many
as fourteen vessels there at one time, and he himself
carried away one hundred thousand skins. It was
a gold mine for profit while it lasted.

There were three Delano brothers afloat in two
vessels, and of their wanderings Amasa set down
this epitome: "Almost the whole of our connec-
tions who were left behind had need of our assistance, and to look forward it was no more than a
reasonable calculation to make that our absence
would not be less than three years . . . together
with the extraordinary uncertainty of the issue
of the voyage, as we had nothing but our hands
to depend upon to obtain a cargo which was only
to be done through storms, dangers, and breakers,
and taken from barren rocks in distant regions.
But after a voyage of four years for one vessel and
five for the other, we were all permitted to return
safe home to our friends and not quite empty-
handed. We had built both of the vessels we were
in and navigated them two and three times around
the globe." Each one of the brothers had been a
master builder and rigger and a navigator of ships
in every part of the world.

By far the most important voyage undertaken by American merchantmen during the decade of brilliant achievement following the Revolution was that of Captain Robert Gray in the *Columbia*, which was the first ship to visit and explore the northwest coast and to lead the way for such adventurers as Richard Cleveland and Amasa Delano. On his second voyage in 1792, Captain Gray discovered the great river he christened Columbia and so gave to the United States its valid title to that vast territory which Lewis and Clark were to find after toiling over the mountains thirteen years later.

CHAPTER VI

"FREE TRADE AND SAILORS' RIGHTS!"

WHEN the first Congress under the new Federal
Constitution assembled in 1789, a spirit of pride
was manifested in the swift recovery and the encouraging growth of the merchant marine, together
with a concerted determination to promote and
protect it by means of national legislation. The
most imperative need was a series of retaliatory
measures to meet the burdensome navigation laws
of England, to give American ships a fair field
and no favors. The Atlantic trade was therefore stimulated by allowing a reduction of ten per
cent of the customs duties on goods imported in
vessels built and owned by American citizens.
The East India trade, which already employed
forty New England ships, was fostered in like
manner. Teas brought direct under the American flag paid an average duty of twelve cents a
pound while teas in foreign bottoms were taxed

twenty-seven cents. It was sturdy protection, for on a cargo of one hundred thousand pounds of assorted teas from India or China, a British ship would pay $27,800 into the custom house and a Salem square-rigger only $10,980.

The result was that the valuable direct trade with the Far East was absolutely secured to the American flag. Not content with this, Congress decreed a system of tonnage duties which permitted the native owner to pay six cents per ton on his vessel while the foreigner laid down fifty cents as an entry fee for every ton his ship measured, or thirty cents if he owned an American-built vessel. In 1794, Congress became even more energetic in defense of its mariners and increased the tariff rates on merchandise in foreign vessels. A nation at last united, jealous of its rights, resentful of indignities long suffered, and intelligently alive to its shipping as the chief bulwark of prosperity, struck back with peaceful weapons and gained a victory of incalculable advantage. Its Congress, no longer feeble and divided, laid the foundations for American greatness upon the high seas which was to endure for more than a half century. Wars, embargoes, and confiscations might interrupt but they could not seriously harm it.

7

In the three years after 1789 the merchant shipping registered for the foreign trade increased from 123,893 tons to 411,438 tons, presaging a growth without parallel in the history of the commercial world. Foreign ships were almost entirely driven out of American ports, and ninety-one per cent of imports and eighty-six per cent of exports were conveyed in vessels built and manned by Americans. Before Congress intervened, English merchantmen had controlled three-fourths of our commerce overseas. When Thomas Jefferson, as Secretary of State, fought down Southern opposition to a retaliatory shipping policy, he uttered a warning which his countrymen were to find still true and apt in the twentieth century: "If we have no seamen, our ships will be useless, consequently our ship timber, iron, and hemp; our shipbuilding will be at an end; ship carpenters will go over to other nations; our young men have no call to the sea; our products, carried in foreign bottoms, will be saddled with war-freight and insurance in time of war — and the history of the last hundred years shows that the nation which is our carrier has three years of war for every four years of peace."

The steady growth of an American merchant

marine was interrupted only once in the following
decade. In the year 1793 war broke out between
England and France. A decree of the National
Convention of the French Republic granted neutral vessels the same rights as those which flew
the tricolor. This privilege reopened a rushing
trade with the West Indies, and hundreds of ships
hastened from American ports to Martinique,
Guadeloupe, and St. Lucia.

Like a thunderbolt came the tidings that England refused to look upon this trade with the
French colonies as neutral and that her cruisers
had been told to seize all vessels engaged in it and
to search them for English-born seamen. This
ruling was enforced with such barbarous severity
that it seemed as if the War for Independence had
been fought in vain. Without warning, unable to
save themselves, great fleets of Yankee merchantmen were literally swept from the waters of the
West Indies. At St. Eustatius one hundred and
thirty of them were condemned. The judges
at Bermuda condemned eleven more. Crews
and passengers were flung ashore without food
or clothing, were abused, insulted, or perhaps impressed in British privateers. The ships were lost
to their owners. There was no appeal and no

redress. At Martinique an English fleet and army captured St. Pierre in February, 1794. Files of marines boarded every American ship in the harbor, tore down the colors, and flung two hundred and fifty seamen into the foul holds of a prison hulk. There they were kept, half-dead with thirst and hunger while their vessels, uncared for, had stranded or sunk at their moorings. Scores of outrages as abominable as this were on record in the office of the Secretary of State. Shipmasters were afraid to sail to the southward and, for lack of these markets for dried cod, the fishing schooners of Marblehead were idle.

For a time a second war with England seemed imminent. An alarmed Congress passed laws to create a navy and to fortify the most important American harbors. President Washington recommended an embargo of thirty days, which Congress promptly voted and then extended for thirty more. It was a popular measure and strictly enforced by the mariners themselves. The mates and captains of the brigs and snows in the Delaware River met and resolved not to go to sea for another ten days, swearing to lie idle sooner than feed the British robbers in the West Indies. It was in the midst of these demonstrations that Washington seized the one hope of peace and recommended a special mission to England.

The treaty negotiated by John Jay in 1794 was received with an outburst of popular indignation. Jay was damned as a traitor, while the sailors of Portsmouth burned him in effigy. By way of an answer to the terms of the obnoxious treaty, a seafaring mob in Boston raided and burned the British privateer *Speedwell*, which had put into that port as a merchantman with her guns and munitions hidden beneath a cargo of West India produce.

The most that can be said of the commercial provisions of the treaty is that they opened direct trade with the East Indies but at the price of complete freedom of trade for British shipping in American ports. It must be said, too, that although the treaty failed to clear away the gravest cause of hostility — the right of search and impressment — yet it served to postpone the actual clash, and during the years in which it was in force American shipping splendidly prospered, freed of its most irksome handicaps.

The quarrel with France had been brewing at the same time and for similar reasons. Neutral trade with England was under the ban, and the

Yankee shipmaster was in danger of losing his
vessel if he sailed to or from a port under the British flag. It was out of the frying-pan into the fire,
and French privateers welcomed the excuse to
go marauding in the Atlantic and the Caribbean.
What it meant to fight off these greedy cutthroats
is told in a newspaper account of the engagement of
Captain Richard Wheatland, who was homeward
bound to Salem in the ship *Perseverance* in 1799.
He was in the Old Straits of Bahama when a fast
schooner came up astern, showing Spanish colors
and carrying a tremendous press of canvas. Unable to run away from her, Captain Wheatland
reported to his owners:

We took in steering sails, wore ship, hauled up our
courses, piped all hands to quarters and prepared for
action. The schooner immediately took in sail, hoisted
an English Union flag and passed under our lee at a considerable distance. We wore ship, she did the same,
and we passed each other within half a musket. A
fellow hailed us in broken English and ordered the boat
hoisted out and the captain to come aboard, which he
refused. He again ordered our boat out and enforced
his orders with a menace that in case of refusal he would
sink us, using at the same time the vilest and most infamous language it is possible to conceive of. . . . We
hauled the ship to wind and as he passed poured a whole
broadside into him with great success. Sailing faster

than we, he ranged considerably ahead, tacked and again passed, giving us a broadside and furious discharge of musketry, which he kept up incessantly until the latter part of the engagement. His musket balls reached us in every direction but his large shot either fell short or went considerably over us while our guns loaded with round shot and square bars of iron were plied so briskly and directed with such good judgment that before he got out of range we had cut his mainsail and foretopsail all to rags and cleared his decks so effectively that when he bore away from us there were scarcely ten men to be seen. He then struck his English flag and hoisted the flag of The Terrible Republic and made off with all the sail he could carry, much disappointed, no doubt, at not being able to give us a fraternal embrace. We feel confidence that we have rid the world of some infamous pests of society.

By this time, the United States was engaged in active hostilities with France, although war had not been declared. The news of the indignities which American commissions had suffered at the hands of the French Directory had stirred the people to war pitch. Strong measures for national defense were taken, which stopped little short of war. The country rallied to the slogan, "Millions for defense but not one cent for tribute," and the merchants of the seaports hastened to subscribe funds to build frigates to be loaned to the Government. Salem launched the famous *Essex*, ready

for sea six months after the keel was laid, at a cost
of $75,000. Her two foremost merchants, Elias
Hasket Derby and William Gray, led the list with
ten thousand dollars each. The call sent out by
the master builder, Enos Briggs, rings with thrilling
effect:

To Sons of Freedom! All true lovers of Liberty of your
Country! Step forth and give your assistance in building the frigate to oppose French insolence and piracy.
Let every man in possession of a white oak tree be ambitious to be foremost in hurrying down the timber to
Salem where the noble structure is to be fabricated to
maintain your rights upon the seas and make the name
of America respected among the nations of the world.
Your largest and longest trees are wanted, and the arms
of them for knees and rising timber. Four trees are
wanted for the keel which altogether will measure 146
feet in length, and hew sixteen inches square.

This handsome frigate privately built by patriots of the republic illuminates the coastwise
spirit and conditions of her time. She was a Salem
ship from keel to truck. Captain Jonathan Haraden, the finest privateersman of the Revolution,
made the rigging for the mainmast at his rope-
walk in Brown Street. Joseph Vincent fitted out
the foremast and Thomas Briggs the mizzenmast
in their lofts at the foot of the Common. When

the huge hemp cables were ready for the frigate, the workmen carried them to the shipyard on their shoulders, the parade led by fife and drum. Her sails were cut from duck woven in Daniel Rust's factory in Broad Street and her iron work was forged by Salem shipsmiths. It was not surprising that Captain Richard Derby was chosen to command the *Essex*, but he was abroad in a ship of his own and she sailed under Captain Edward Preble of the Navy.

The war cloud passed and the merchant argosies overflowed the wharves and havens of New England, which had ceased to monopolize the business on blue water. New York had become a seaport with long ranks of high-steeved bowsprits soaring above pleasant Battery Park and a forest of spars extending up the East River. In 1790 more than two thousand ships, brigs, schooners, and smaller craft had entered and cleared, and the merchants met in the coffee-houses to discuss charters, bills-of-lading, and adventures. Sailors commanded thrice the wages of laborers ashore. Shipyards were increasing and the builders could build as large and swift East Indiamen as those of which Boston and Salem boasted.

Philadelphia had her Stephen Girard, whose

wealth was earned in ships, a man most remarkable and eccentric, whose career was one of the great maritime romances. Though his father was a prosperous merchant of Bordeaux engaged in the West India trade, he was shifting for himself as a cabin-boy on his father's ships when only fourteen years old. With no schooling, barely able to read and write, this urchin sailed between Bordeaux and the French West Indies for nine years, until he gained the rank of first mate. At the age of twenty-six he entered the port of Philadelphia in command of a sloop which had narrowly escaped capture by British frigates. There he took up his domicile and laid the foundation of his fortune in small trading ventures to New Orleans and Santo Domingo.

In 1791 he began to build a fleet of beautiful ships for the China and India trade, their names, *Montesquieu, Helvétius, Voltaire*, and *Rousseau*, revealing his ideas of religion and liberty. So successfully did he combine banking and shipping that in 1813 he was believed to be the wealthiest merchant in the United States. In that year one of his ships from China was captured off the Capes of the Delaware by a British privateer. Her cargo of teas, nankeens, and silks was worth half a

STEPHEN GIRARD

Engraving by J. Cheney.

million dollars to him but he succeeded in ransoming it on the spot by counting out one hundred and eighty thousand Spanish milled dollars. No privateersman could resist such strategy as this.

Alone in his old age, without a friend or relative to close his eyes in death, Stephen Girard, once a penniless, ignorant French cabin-boy, bequeathed his millions to philanthropy, and the Girard College for orphan boys, in Philadelphia, is his monument.

The Treaty of Amiens brought a little respite to Europe and a peaceful interlude for American shipmasters, but France and England came to grips again in 1803. For two years thereafter the United States was almost the only important neutral nation not involved in the welter of conflict on land and sea, and trade everywhere sought the protection of the Stars and Stripes. England had swept her own rivals, men-of-war and merchantmen, from the face of the waters. France and Holland ceased to carry cargoes beneath their own ensigns. Spain was afraid to send her galleons to Mexico and Peru. All the Continental ports were begging for American ships to transport their merchandise. It was a maritime harvest unique and unexpected.

Yankee skippers were dominating the sugar trade of Cuba and were rolling across the Atlantic with the coffee, hides, and indigo of Venezuela and Brazil. Their fleets crowded the roadsteads of Manila and Batavia and packed the warehouses of Antwerp, Lisbon, and Hamburg. It was a situation which England could not tolerate without attempting to thwart an immense traffic which she construed as giving aid and comfort to her enemies. Under cover of the so-called Rule of 1756 British admiralty courts began to condemn American vessels carrying products from enemies' colonies to Europe, even when the voyage was broken by first entering an American port. It was on record in September, 1805, that fifty American ships had been condemned in England and as many more in the British West Indies.

This was a trifling disaster, however, compared with the huge calamity which befell when Napoleon entered Berlin as a conqueror and proclaimed his paper blockade of the British Isles. There was no French navy to enforce it, but American vessels dared not sail for England lest they be snapped up by French privateers. The British Government savagely retaliated with further prohibitions, and Napoleon countered in like manner until no sea was safe for a neutral ship and the United States was powerless to assert its rights. Thomas Jefferson as President used as a weapon the Embargo of 1807, which was, at first, a popular measure, and which he justified in these pregnant sentences: "The whole world is thus laid under interdict by these two nations, and our own vessels, their cargoes, and crews, are to be taken by the one or the other for whatever place they may be destined out of our limits. If, therefore, on leaving our harbors we are certainly to lose them, is it not better as to vessels, cargoes, and seamen, to keep them at home?"

A people proud, independent, and pugnacious, could not long submit to a measure of defense which was, in the final sense, an abject surrender to brute force. New England, which bore the brunt of the embargo, was first to rebel against it. Sailors marched through the streets clamoring for bread or loaded their vessels and fought their way to sea. In New York the streets of the waterside were deserted, ships dismantled, counting-houses unoccupied, and warehouses empty. In one year foreign commerce decreased in value from $108,-000,000 to $22,000,000.

After fifteen months Congress repealed the law,

substituting a Non-Intercourse Act which sus-
pended trade with Great Britain and France until
their offending orders were repealed. All such
measures were doomed to be futile. Words and
documents, threats and arguments could not in-
timidate adversaries who paid heed to nothing
else than broadsides from line-of-battle ships or the
charge of battalions. With other countries trade
could now be opened. Hopefully the hundreds
of American ships long pent-up in harbor winged
it deep-laden for the Baltic, the North Sea, and the
Mediterranean. But few of them ever returned.
Like a brigand, Napoleon lured them into a trap
and closed it, advising the Prussian Government,
which was under his heel: "Let the American
ships enter your ports. Seize them afterward.
You shall deliver the cargoes to me and I will take
them in part payment of the Prussian war debt."

Similar orders were executed wherever his
mailed fist reached, the pretext being reprisal for
the Non-Intercourse Act. More than two hundred American vessels were lost to their owners, a
ten-million-dollar robbery for which France paid
an indemnity of five millions after twenty years.
It was the grand climax of the exploitation which
American commerce had been compelled to endure

through two centuries of tumult and bloodshed afloat. There lingers today in many a coastwise town an inherited dislike for France. It is a legacy of that far-off catastrophe which beggared many a household and filled the streets with haggard, broken shipmasters.

It was said of this virile merchant marine that it throve under pillage and challenged confiscation. Statistics confirm this brave paradox. In 1810, while Napoleon was doing his worst, the deep-sea tonnage amounted to 981,019; and it is a singular fact that in proportion to population this was to stand as the high tide of American foreign shipping until thirty-seven years later. It ebbed during the War of 1812 but rose again with peace and a real and lasting freedom of the seas.

This second war with England was fought in behalf of merchant seamen and they played a nobly active part in it. The ruthless impressment of seamen was the most conspicuous provocation, but it was only one of many. Two years before hostilities were openly declared, British frigates were virtually blockading the port of New York, halting and searching ships as they pleased, making prizes of those with French destinations, stealing sailors to fill their crews, waging war in everything but name, and enjoying the sport of it. A midshipman of one of them merrily related: "Every morning at daybreak we set about arresting the progress of all the vessels we saw, firing off guns to the right and left to make every ship that was running in heave to or wait until we had leisure to send a boat on board to see, in our lingo, what she was made of. I have frequently known a dozen and sometimes a couple of dozen ships lying a league or two off the port, losing their fair wind, their tide, and worse than all, their market for many hours, sometimes the whole day, before our search was completed."

The right of a belligerent to search neutral vessels for contraband of war or evidence of a forbidden destination was not the issue at stake. This was a usage sanctioned by such international law as then existed. It was the alleged right to search for English seamen in neutral vessels that Great Britain exercised, not only on the high seas but even in territorial waters, which the American Government refused to recognize. In vain the Government had endeavored to protect its sailors from impressment by means of certificates of birth and citizenship. These documents were jeered at by the English naval lieutenant and his boarding gang, who kidnapped from the forecastle such stalwart tars as pleased their fancy. The victim who sought to inform an American consul of his plight was lashed to the rigging and flogged by a boatswain's mate. The files of the State Department, in 1807, had contained the names of six thousand American sailors who were as much slaves and prisoners aboard British men-of-war as if they had been made captives by the Dey of Algiers. One of these incidents, occurring on the ship *Betsy*, Captain Nathaniel Silsbee, while at Madras in 1795, will serve to show how this brutal business was done.

I received a note early one morning from my chief mate that one of my sailors, Edward Hulen, a fellow townsman whom I had known from boyhood, had been impressed and taken on board of a British frigate then lying in port. . . . I immediately went on board my ship and having there learned all the facts in the case, proceeded to the frigate, where I found Hulen and in his presence was informed by the first lieutenant of the frigate that he had taken Hulen from my ship under a peremptory order from his commander to visit every American ship in port and take from each of them one or more of their seamen. . . . I then called upon Captain Cook, who commanded the frigate, and sought first by all the persuasive means that I was capable of using and ultimately by threats to appeal to the Government of the place to obtain Hulen's release, but in

8

vain. . . . It remained for me only to recommend Hulen to that protection of the lieutenant which a good seaman deserves, and to submit to the high-handed insult thus offered to the flag of my country which I had no means either of preventing or resisting.

After several years' detention in the British Navy, Hulen returned to Salem and lived to serve on board privateers in the second war with England.

Several years' detention! This was what it meant to be a pressed man, perhaps with wife and children at home who had no news of him nor any wages to support them. At the time of the Nore Mutiny in 1797, there were ships in the British fleet whose men had not been paid off for eight, ten, twelve, and in one instance fifteen years. These wooden walls of England were floating hells, and a seaman was far better off in jail. He was flogged if he sulked and again if he smiled — flogged until the blood ran for a hundred offenses as trivial as these. His food was unspeakably bad and often years passed before he was allowed to set foot ashore. Decent men refused to volunteer and the ships were filled with the human scum and refuse caught in the nets of the press-gangs of Liverpool, London, and Bristol.

It is largely forgotten or unknown that this

system of recruiting was as intolerable in England as it was in the United States and as fiercely resented. Oppressive and unjust, it was nevertheless endured as the bulwark of England's defense against her foes. It ground under its heel the very people it protected and made them serfs in order to keep them free. No man of the common people who lived near the coast of England was safe from the ruffianly press-gangs nor any merchant ship that entered her ports. It was the most cruel form of conscription ever devised. Mob violence opposed it again and again, and British East Indiamen fought the King's tenders sooner than be stripped of their crews and left helpless. Feeling in America against impressment was never more highly inflamed, even on the brink of the War of 1812, than it had long been in England itself, although the latter country was unable to rise and throw it off. Here are the words, not of an angry American patriot but of a modern English historian writing of his own nation:[1] "To the people the impress was an axe laid at the foot of the tree. There was here no question, as with trade, of the mere loss of hands who could be replaced. Attacking the family in the person of its natural

[1] *The Press Gang Afloat and Ashore*, by J. R. Hutchinson.

supporter and protector, the octopus system of which the gangs were the tentacles, struck at the very foundations of domestic life and brought to thousands of households a poverty as bitter and a grief as poignant as death. . . . The mutiny at the Nore brought the people face to face with the appalling risks attendant on wholesale pressing while the war with America, incurred for the sole purpose of upholding the right to press, taught them the lengths to which their rulers were still prepared to go in order to enslave them."

CHAPTER VII

THE BRILLIANT ERA OF 1812

AMERICAN privateering in 1812 was even bolder and more successful than during the Revolution. It was the work of a race of merchant seamen who had found themselves, who were in the forefront of the world's trade and commerce, and who were equipped to challenge the enemy's pretensions to supremacy afloat. Once more there was a mere shadow of a navy to protect them, but they had learned to trust their own resources. They would send to sea fewer of the small craft, slow and poorly armed, and likely to meet disaster. They were capable of manning what was, in fact, a private navy comprised of fast and formidable cruisers. The intervening generation had advanced the art of building and handling ships beyond all rivalry, and England grudgingly acknowledged their ability. The year of 1812 was indeed but a little distance from the resplendent modern

117

era of the Atlantic packet and the Cape Horn
clipper.

Already these Yankee deep-water ships could be
recognized afar by their lofty spars and snowy
clouds of cotton duck beneath which the slender
hull was a thin black line. Far up to the gleaming royals they carried sail in winds so strong that
the lumbering English East Indiamen were hove
to or snugged down to reefed topsails. It was not
recklessness but better seamanship. The deeds
of the Yankee privateers of 1812 prove this asser-
tion to the hilt. Their total booty amounted to
thirteen hundred prizes taken over all the Seven
Seas, with a loss to England of forty million dollars
in ships and cargoes. There were, all told, more
than five hundred of them in commission, but New
England no longer monopolized this dashing trade.
Instead of Salem it was Baltimore that furnished
the largest fleet — fifty-eight vessels, many of
them the fast ships and schooners which were to
make the port famous as the home of the Baltimore clipper model. All down the coast, out of
Norfolk, Wilmington, Charleston, Savannah, and
New Orleans, sallied the privateers to show that
theirs was, in truth, a seafaring nation ardently
united in a common cause.

Again and more vehemently the people of England raised their voices in protest and lament, for these saucy sea-raiders fairly romped to and fro in the Channel, careless of pursuit, conducting a blockade of their own until London was paying the famine price of fifty-eight dollars a barrel for flour, and it was publicly declared mortifying and distressing that "a horde of American cruisers should be allowed, unresisted and unmolested, to take, burn, or sink our own vessels in our own inlets and almost in sight of our own harbors." It was Captain Thomas Boyle in the *Chasseur* of Baltimore who impudently sent ashore his proclamation of a blockade of the United Kingdom of Great Britain and Ireland, which he requested should be posted in Lloyd's Coffee House.

A wonderfully fine figure of a fighting seaman was this Captain Boyle, with an Irish sense of humor which led him to haunt the enemy's coast and to make sport of the frigates which tried to catch him. His *Chasseur* was considered one of the ablest privateers of the war and the most beautiful vessel ever seen in Baltimore. A fleet and graceful schooner with a magical turn for speed, she mounted sixteen long twelve-pounders and carried a hundred officers, seamen, and marines, and was never outsailed in fair winds or foul. "Out of sheer wantonness," said an admirer, "she sometimes affected to chase the enemy's men-of-war of far superior force." Once when surrounded by two frigates and two naval brigs, she slipped through and was gone like a phantom. During his first cruise in the *Chasseur*, Captain Boyle captured eighteen valuable merchantmen. It was such defiant rovers as he that provoked the *Morning Chronicle* of London to splutter "that the whole coast of Ireland from Wexford round by Cape Clear to Carrickfergus, should have been for above a month under the unresisted domination of a few petty fly-by-nights from the blockaded ports of the United States is a grievance equally intolerable and disgraceful."

This was when the schooner *Syren* had captured His Majesty's cutter *Landrail* while crossing the Irish Sea with dispatches; when the *Governor Tompkins* burned fourteen English vessels in the English Channel in quick succession; when the *Harpy* of Baltimore cruised for three months off the Irish and English coasts and in the Bay of Biscay and returned to Boston filled with spoils, including a half million dollars of money; when the *Prince de Neuchâtel* hovered at her leisure in the Irish

Channel and made coasting trade impossible; and when the *Young Wasp* of Philadelphia cruised for six months in those same waters.

Two of the privateers mentioned were first-class fighting ships whose engagements were as notable, in their way, as those of the American frigates which made the war as illustrious by sea as it was ignominious by land. While off Havana in 1815, Captain Boyle met the schooner *St. Lawrence* of the British Navy, a fair match in men and guns. The *Chasseur* could easily have run away but stood up to it and shot the enemy to pieces in fifteen minutes. Brave and courteous were these two commanders, and Lieutenant Gordon of the *St. Lawrence* gave his captor a letter which read, in part: "In the event of Captain Boyle's becoming a prisoner of war to any British cruiser I consider it a tribute justly due to his humane and generous treatment of myself, the surviving officers, and crew of His Majesty's late schooner *St. Lawrence*, to state that his obliging attention and watchful solicitude to preserve our effects and render us comfortable during the short time we were in his possession were such as justly entitle him to the indulgence and respect of every British subject."

The *Prince de Neuchâtel* had the honor of beating

off the attack of a forty-gun British frigate — an exploit second only to that of the *General Armstrong* in the harbor of Fayal. This privateer with a foreign name hailed from New York and was so fortunate as to capture for her owners three million dollars' worth of British merchandise. With Captain J. Ordronaux on the quarter-deck, she was near Nantucket Shoals at noon on October 11, 1814, when a strange sail was discovered. As this vessel promptly gave chase, Captain Ordronaux guessed — and as events proved correctly — that she must be a British frigate. She turned out to be the *Endymion*. The privateer had in tow a prize which she was anxious to get into port, but she was forced to cast off the hawser late in the afternoon and make every effort to escape.

The breeze died with the sun and the vessels were close inshore. Becalmed, the privateer and the frigate anchored a quarter of a mile apart. Captain Ordronaux might have put his crew on the beach in boats and abandoned his ship. This was the reasonable course, for, as he had sent in several prize crews, he was short-handed and could muster no more than thirty-seven men and boys. The *Endymion*, on the other hand, had a complement of three hundred and fifty sailors and marines, and in size and fighting power she was in the class of the American frigates *President* and *Constitution*. Quite unreasonably, however, the master of the privateer decided to await events.

The unexpected occurred shortly after dusk when several boats loaded to the gunwales with a boarding party crept away from the frigate. Five of them, with one hundred and twenty men, made a concerted attack at different points, alongside and under the bow and stern. Captain Ordronaux had told his crew that he would blow up the ship with all hands before striking his colors, and they believed him implicitly. This was the hero who was described as "a Jew by persuasion, a Frenchman by birth, an American for convenience, and so diminutive in stature as to make him appear ridiculous, in the eyes of others, even for him to enforce authority among a hardy, weather-beaten crew should they do aught against his will." He was big enough, nevertheless, for this night's bloody work, and there was no doubt about his authority. While the British tried to climb over the bulwarks, his thirty-seven men and boys fought like raging devils, with knives, pistols, cutlases, with their bare fists and their teeth. A few of the enemy gained the deck, but the privateersmen turned and killed them. Others leaped aboard and were gradually driving the Americans back, when the skipper ran to the hatch above the powder magazine, waving a lighted match and swearing to drop it in if his crew retreated one step further. Either way the issue seemed desperate. But again they took their skipper's word for it and rallied for a bloody struggle which soon swept the decks.

No more than twenty minutes had passed and the battle was won. The enemy was begging for quarter. One boat had been sunk, three had drifted away filled with dead and wounded, and the fifth was captured with thirty-six men in it of whom only eight were unhurt. The American loss was seven killed and twenty-four wounded, or thirty-one of her crew of thirty-seven. Yet they had not given up the ship. The frigate *Endymion* concluded that once was enough, and next morning the *Prince de Neuchâtel* bore away for Boston with a freshening breeze.

Those were merchant seamen also who held the *General Armstrong* against a British squadron through that moonlit night in Fayal Roads, inflicting heavier losses than were suffered in any naval action of the war. It is a story Homeric, almost incredible in its details and so often repeated that it can be only touched upon in this brief chronicle. The leader was a kindly featured man who wore a tall hat, side-whiskers, and a tail coat. His portrait might easily have served for that of a New England deacon of the old school. No trace of the swashbuckler in this Captain Samuel Reid, who had been a thrifty, respected merchant skipper until offered the command of a privateer.

Touching at the Azores for water and provisions in September, 1814, he was trapped in port by the great seventy-four-gun ship of the line *Plantagenet*, the thirty-eight-gun frigate *Rota*, and the war-brig *Carnation*. Though he was in neutral water, they paid no heed to this but determined to destroy a Yankee schooner which had played havoc with their shipping. Four hundred men in twelve boats, with a howitzer in the bow of each boat, were sent against the *General Armstrong* in one flotilla. But not a man of the four hundred gained her deck. Said an eyewitness: "The Americans fought with great firmness but more like blood-thirsty savages than anything else. They rushed into the boats sword in hand and put every soul to death as far as came within their power. Some of the boats were left without a single man to row them, others with three or four. The most that any one returned with was about ten. Several boats floated ashore full of dead bodies. . . . For three days after the battle we were employed in burying the dead that washed on shore in the surf."

This tragedy cost the British squadron one hundred and twenty men in killed and one hundred and thirty in wounded, while Captain Reid lost only two dead and had seven wounded. He was compelled to retreat ashore next day when the ships stood in to sink his schooner with their big guns, but the honors of war belonged to him and well-earned were the popular tributes when he saw home again, nor was there a word too much in the florid toast: "Captain Reid — his valor has shed a blaze of renown upon the character of our seamen, and won for himself a laurel of eternal bloom."

It is not to glorify war nor to rekindle an ancient feud that such episodes as these are recalled to mind. These men, and others like them, did their duty as it came to them, and they were sailors of whom the whole Anglo-Saxon race might be proud. In the crisis they were Americans, not privateersmen in quest of plunder, and they would gladly die sooner than haul down the Stars and Stripes. The England against which they fought was not the England of today. Their honest grievances, inflicted by a Government too intent upon crushing Napoleon to be fair to neutrals, have long ago been obliterated. This War of 1812 cleared the vision of the Mother Country and forever taught her Government that the people of the Republic were, in truth, free and independent.

This lesson was driven home not only by the guns of the *Constitution* and the *United States*, but also by the hundreds of privateers and the forty thousand able seamen who were eager to sail in them. They found no great place in naval history, but England knew their prowess and respected it. Every schoolboy is familiar with the duels of the *Wasp* and the *Frolic*, of the *Enterprise* and the *Boxer;* but how many people know what happened when the privateer *Decatur* met and whipped the *Dominica* of the British Navy to the southward of Bermuda?

Captain Diron was the man who did it as he was cruising out of Charleston, South Carolina, in the summer of 1813. Sighting an armed schooner slightly heavier than his own vessel, he made for her and was unperturbed when the royal ensign streamed from her gaff. Clearing for action, he closed the hatches so that none of his men could hide below. The two schooners fought in the veiling smoke until the American could ram her bowsprit over the other's stern and pour her whole crew aboard. In the confined space of the deck, almost two hundred men and lads were slashing and stabbing and shooting amid yells and huzzas. Lieutenant Barretté, the English commander, only twenty-five years old, was mortally hurt and every other officer, excepting the surgeon and one midshipman, was killed or wounded. Two-thirds of the crew were down but still they refused to surrender, and Captain Diron had to pull down the colors with his own hands. Better discipline and marksmanship had won the day for him and his losses were comparatively small.

Men of his description were apt to think first of glory and let the profits go hang, for there was no cargo to be looted in a King's ship. Other privateersmen, however, were not so valiant or quarrelsome, and there was many a one tied up in London River or the Mersey which had been captured without very savage resistance. Yet on the whole it is fair to say that the private armed ships

CAPTAIN JAMES CHEEVER, OF THE PRIVATEER
"AMERICA"

Photograph from a crayon drawing given by Charles G. Cheever, Andover, Massachusetts, to the Peabody Museum, Salem, Massachusetts.

THE SHIP "AMERICA"

The fourth of her name. Privateer in the War of 1812. Watercolor drawing by Antoine Roux, Marseilles, 1806. In the Peabody Museum, Salem, Massachusetts.

outfought and outsailed the enemy as impressively as did the few frigates of the American Navy.

There was a class of them which exemplified the rapid development of the merchant marine in a conspicuous manner — large commerce destroyers too swift to be caught, too powerful to fear the smaller cruisers. They were extremely profitable business ventures, entrusted to the command of the most audacious and skillful masters that could be engaged. Of this type was the ship *America* of Salem, owned by the Crowninshields, which made twenty-six prizes and brought safely into port property which realized more than a million dollars. Of this the owners and shareholders received six hundred thousand dollars as dividends. She was a stately vessel, built for the East India trade, and was generally conceded to be the fastest privateer afloat. For this service the upper deck was removed and the sides were filled in with stout oak timber as an armored protection, and longer yards and royal masts gave her a huge area of sail. Her crew of one hundred and fifty men had the exacting organization of a man-of-war, including, it is interesting to note, three lieutenants, three mates, a sailing-master, surgeon, purser, captain of marines, gunners, seven prize masters, armorer, drummer,

and a fifer. Discipline was severe, and flogging was
the penalty for breaking the regulations.

During her four cruises, the *America* swooped
among the plodding merchantmen like a falcon on
a dovecote, the sight of her frightening most of
her prey into submission, with a brush now and
then to exercise the crews of the twenty-two guns,
and perhaps a man or two hit. Long after the war,
Captain James Chever, again a peaceful merchant
mariner, met at Valparaiso, Sir James Thompson,
commander of the British frigate *Dublin*, which
had been fitted out in 1813 for the special purpose of chasing the *America*. In the course of a
cordial chat between the two captains the Briton
remarked:

"I was once almost within gun-shot of that in-
fernal Yankee skimming-dish, just as night came
on. By daylight she had outsailed the *Dublin* so
devilish fast that she was no more than a speck on
the horizon. By the way, I wonder if you happen
to know the name of the beggar that was master
of her."

"I'm the beggar," chuckled Captain Chever,
and they drank each other's health on the strength
of it.

Although the Treaty of Ghent omitted mention

of the impressment of sailors, which had been the burning issue of the war, there were no more offenses of this kind. American seafarers were safe against kidnapping on their own decks, and they had won this security by virtue of their own double-shotted guns. At the same time England lifted the curse of the press-gang from her own people, who refused longer to endure it.

There seemed no reason why the two nations, having finally fought their differences to a finish, should not share the high seas in peaceful rivalry; but the irritating problems of protection and reciprocity survived to plague and hamper commerce. It was difficult for England to overcome the habit of guarding her trade against foreign invasion. Agreeing with the United States to waive all discriminating duties between the ports of the two countries — this was as much as she was at that time willing to yield. She still insisted upon regulating the trade of her West Indies and Canada. American East Indiamen were to be limited to direct voyages and could not bring cargoes to Europe. Though this discrimination angered Congress, to which it appeared as lopsided reciprocity, the old duties were nevertheless repealed; and then, presto! the British colonial policy of exclusion was enforced and eighty thousand tons of American shipping became idle because the West India market was closed.

There followed several years of unhappy wrangling, a revival of the old smuggling spirit, the risk of seizure and confiscations, and shipping merchants with long faces talking ruin. The theory of free trade versus protection was as debatable and opinions were as conflicting then as now. Some were for retaliation, others for conciliation; and meanwhile American shipmasters went about their business, with no room for theories in their honest heads, and secured more and more of the world's trade. Curiously enough, the cries of calamity in the United States were echoed across the water, where the *London Times* lugubriously exclaimed: "The shipping interest, the cradle of our navy, is half ruined. Our commercial monopoly exists no longer; and thousands of our manufacturers are starving or seeking redemption in distant lands. We have closed the Western Indies against America from feelings of commercial rivalry. Its active seamen have already engrossed an important branch of our carrying trade to the Eastern Indies. Her starred flag is now conspicuous on every sea and will soon defy our thunder."

It was not until 1849 that Great Britain threw overboard her long catalogue of protective navigation laws which had been piling up since the time of Cromwell, and declared for free trade afloat. Meanwhile the United States had drifted in the same direction, barring foreign flags from its coastwise shipping but offering full exemption from all discriminating duties and tonnage duties to every maritime nation which should respond in like manner. This latter legislation was enacted in 1828 and definitely abandoned the doctrine of protection in so far as it applied to American ships and sailors. For a generation thereafter, during which ocean rivalry was a battle royal of industry, enterprise, and skill, the United States was paramount and her merchant marine attained its greatest successes.

There is one school of modern economists who hold that the seeds of decay and downfall were planted by this adoption of free trade in 1828, while another faction of gentlemen quite as estimable and authoritative will quote facts and figures by the ream to prove that governmental policies had nothing whatever to do with the case. These adversaries have written and are still writing many volumes in which they almost invariably lose their tempers. Partisan politics befog the tariff issue afloat as well as ashore, and one's course is not easy to chart. It is indisputable, however, that so long as Yankee ships were better, faster, and more economically managed, they won a commanding share of the world's trade. When they ceased to enjoy these qualities of superiority, they lost the trade and suffered for lack of protection to overcome the handicap.

The War of 1812 was the dividing line between two eras of salt water history. On the farther side lay the turbulent centuries of hazard and bloodshed and piracy, of little ships and indomitable seamen who pursued their voyages in the reek of gunpowder and of legalized pillage by the stronger, and of merchant adventurers who explored new markets wherever there was water enough to float their keels. They belonged to the rude and lusty youth of a world which lived by the sword and which gloried in action. Even into the early years of the nineteenth century these mariners still sailed — Elizabethan in deed and spirit.

On the hither side of 1812 were seas unvexed by the privateer and the freebooter. The lateen-rigged corsairs had been banished from their lairs in the harbors of Algiers, and ships needed to show no broadsides of cannon in the Atlantic trade. For a time they carried the old armament among the lawless islands of the Orient and off Spanish-American coasts where the vocation of piracy made its last stand, but the great trade routes of the globe were peaceful highways for the white-winged fleets of all nations. The American seamen who had fought for the right to use the open sea were now to display their prowess in another way and in a romance of achievement that was no less large and thrilling.

CHAPTER VIII

THE PACKET SHIPS OF THE "ROARING FORTIES"

IT was on the stormy Atlantic, called by sailormen the Western Ocean, that the packet ships won the first great contest for supremacy and knew no rivals until the coming of the age of steam made them obsolete. Their era antedated that of the clipper and was wholly distinct. The Atlantic packet was the earliest liner: she made regular sailings and carried freight and passengers instead of trading on her owners' account as was the ancient custom. Not for her the tranquillity of tropic seas and the breath of the Pacific trades, but an almost incessant battle with swinging surges and boisterous winds, for she was driven harder in all weathers and seasons than any other ships that sailed. In such battering service as this the lines of the clipper were too extremely fine, her spars too tall and slender. The packet was by no means slow and if the list of her record passages

SOUTH STREET, FROM MAIDEN LANE, NEW YORK, 1834

Engraving by W. I. Bennett, from a drawing by himself.   In the Print
Department of the New York Public Library.

was superb, it was because they were accomplished
by masters who would sooner let a sail blow away
than take it in and who raced each other every inch
of the way.

They were small ships of three hundred to five
hundred tons when the famous Black Ball Line
was started in 1816. From the first they were the
ablest vessels that could be built, full-bodied and
stoutly rigged. They were the only regular means
of communication between the United States and
Europe and were entrusted with the mails, specie,
government dispatches, and the lives of eminent
personages. Blow high, blow low, one of the Black
Ball packets sailed from New York for Liverpool
on the first and sixteenth of every month. Other
lines were soon competing — the Red Star and the
Swallow Tail out of New York, and fine ships from
Boston and Philadelphia. With the completion of
the Erie Canal in 1825 the commercial greatness of
New York was assured, and her Atlantic packets
increased in size and numbers, averaging a thousand tons each in the zenith of their glory.

England, frankly confessing herself beaten and
unable to compete with such ships as these,
changed her attitude from hostility to open admiration. She surrendered the Atlantic packet

trade to American enterprise, and British merchantmen sought their gains in other waters. The
Navigation Laws still protected their commerce
in the Far East and they were content to jog at
a more sedate gait than these weltering packets
whose skippers were striving for passages of a fortnight, with the forecastle doors nailed fast and the
crew compelled to stay on deck from Sandy Hook
to Fastnet Rock.

No blustering, rum-drinking tarpaulin was the
captain who sailed the *Independence*, the *Ocean
Queen*, or the *Dreadnought* but a man very careful
of his manners and his dress, who had been selected
from the most highly educated merchant service in
the world. He was attentive to the comfort of his
passengers and was presumed to have no other
duties on deck than to give the proper orders to his
first officer and work out his daily reckoning. It
was an exacting, nerve-racking ordeal, however,
demanding a sleepless vigilance, courage, and cool
judgment of the first order. The compensations
were large. As a rule, he owned a share of the
ship and received a percentage of the freights and
passage money. His rank when ashore was more
exalted than can be conveyed in mere words. Any
normal New York boy would sooner have been

captain of a Black Ball packet than President of
the United States, and he knew by heart the roaring chantey:

> It is of a flash packet,
>   A packet of fame.
> She is bound to New York
>   And the *Dreadnought's* her name.
> She is bound to the west'ard
>   Where the stormy winds blow.
> Bound away to the west'ard,
>   Good Lord, let her go.

There were never more than fifty of these ships
afloat, a trifling fraction of the American deep-
water tonnage of that day, but the laurels they
won were immortal. Not only did the English
mariner doff his hat to them, but a Parliamentary
committee reported in 1837 that "the American
ships frequenting the ports of England are stated
by several witnesses to be superior to those of a
similar class among the ships of Great Britain, the
commanders and officers being generally considered to be more competent as seamen and navigators and more uniformly persons of education
than the commanders and officers of British ships
of a similar size and class trading from England to
America."

It was no longer a rivalry with the flags of other nations but an unceasing series of contests among the packets of the several lines, and their records aroused far more popular excitement than when the great steamers of this century were chipping off the minutes, at an enormous coal consumption, toward a five-day passage. Theirs were tests of real seamanship, and there were few disasters. The packet captain scorned a towboat to haul him into the stream if the wind served fair to set all plain sail as his ship lay at her wharf. Driving her stern foremost, he braced his yards and swung her head to sea, clothing the masts with soaring canvas amid the farewell cheers of the crowds which lined the waterfront.

A typical match race was sailed between the Black Ball liner *Columbus*, Captain De Peyster, and the *Sheridan*, Captain Russell, of the splendid Dramatic fleet, in 1837. The stake was $10,000 a side, put up by the owners and their friends. The crews were picked men who were promised a bonus of fifty dollars each for winning. The ships sailed side by side in February, facing the wild winter passage, and the *Columbus* reached Liverpool in the remarkable time of sixteen days, two days ahead of the *Sheridan*.

The crack packets were never able to reel off more than twelve or fourteen knots under the most favorable conditions, but they were kept going night and day, and some of them maintained their schedules almost with the regularity of the early steamers. The *Montezuma*, the *Patrick Henry*, and the *Southampton* crossed from New York to Liverpool in fifteen days, and for years the *Independence* held the record of fourteen days and six hours. It remained for the *Dreadnought*, Captain Samuel Samuels, in 1859, to set the mark for packet ships to Liverpool at thirteen days and eight hours.

Meanwhile the era of the matchless clipper had arrived and it was one of these ships which achieved the fastest Atlantic passage ever made by a vessel under sail. The *James Baines* was built for English owners to be used in the Australian trade. She was a full clipper of 2515 tons, twice the size of the ablest packets, and was praised as "the most perfect sailing ship that ever entered the river Mersey." Bound out from Boston to Liverpool, she anchored after twelve days and six hours at sea.

There was no lucky chance in this extraordinary voyage, for this clipper was the work of the

greatest American builder, Donald McKay, who at
the same time designed the *Lightning* for the same
owners. This clipper, sent across the Atlantic on
her maiden trip, left in her foaming wake a twenty-
four hour run which no steamer had even ap-
proached and which was not equaled by the fastest
express steamers until twenty-five years later when
the greyhound *Arizona* ran eighteen knots in one
hour on her trial trip. This is a rather startling
statement when one reflects that the *Arizona* of
the Guion line seems to a generation still living
a modern steamer and record-holder. It is even
more impressive when coupled with the fact that, of
the innumerable passenger steamers traversing the
seas today, only a few are capable of a speed of
more than eighteen knots.

This clipper *Lightning* did her 436 sea miles in
one day, or eighteen and a half knots, better than
twenty land miles an hour, and this is how the surpassing feat was entered in her log, or official
journal: "March 1. Wind south. Strong gales;
bore away for the North Channel, carrying away
the foretopsail and lost jib; hove the log several
times and found the ship going through the water
at the rate of 18 to 18½ knots; lee rail under water
and rigging slack. Distance run in twenty-four

hours, 436 miles." The passage was remarkably
fast, thirteen days and nineteen and a half hours
from Boston Light, but the spectacular feature
was this day's work. It is a fitting memorial of
the Yankee clipper, and, save only a cathedral, the
loveliest, noblest fabric ever wrought by man's
handiwork.

The clipper, however, was a stranger in the
Atlantic and her chosen courses were elsewhere.
The records made by the *James Baines* and the
Lightning were no discredit to the stanch, unconquerable packet ships which, year in and year out,
held their own with the steamer lines until just
before the Civil War. It was the boast of Captain
Samuels that on her first voyage in 1853 the *Dreadnought* reached Sandy Hook as the Cunarder
Canada, which had left Liverpool a day ahead of
her, was passing in by Boston Light. Twice she
carried the latest news to Europe, and many
seasoned travelers preferred her to the mail
steamers.

The masters and officers who handled these ships
with such magnificent success were true-blue American seamen, inspired by the finest traditions, suc-
cessors of the privateersmen of 1812. The forecastles, however, were filled with English, Irish,

and Scandinavians. American lads shunned these ships and, in fact, the ambitious youngster of the coastwise towns began to cease following the sea almost a century ago. It is sometimes forgotten that the period during which the best American manhood sought a maritime career lay between the Revolution and the War of 1812. Thereafter the story became more and more one of American ships and less of American sailors, excepting on the quarter-deck.

In later years the Yankee crews were to be found in the ports where the old customs survived, the long trading voyage, the community of interest in cabin and forecastle, all friends and neighbors together, with opportunities for profit and advancement. Such an instance was that of the Salem ship *George*, built at Salem in 1814 and owned by the great merchant, Joseph Peabody. For twenty-two years she sailed in the East India trade, making twenty-one round voyages, with an astonishing regularity which would be creditable for a modern cargo tramp. Her sailors were native-born, seldom more than twenty-one years old, and most of them were studying navigation. Forty-five of them became shipmasters, twenty of them chief mates, and six second mates. This reliable

THE SHIP "GEORGE," OF SALEM

Water-color painting, 1820, owned by George H. Allen, Manchester-by-the-Sea. The *George*, 318 tons, was built in 1814, and made twenty voyages between Salem and Calcutta.

George was, in short, a nautical training-school of the best kind and any young seaman with the right stuff in him was sure of advancement.

Seven thousand sailors signed articles in the counting-room of Joseph Peabody and went to sea in his eighty ships which flew the house-flag in Calcutta, Canton, Sumatra, and the ports of Europe until 1844. These were mostly New England boys who followed in the footsteps of their fathers because deep-water voyages were still "adventures" and a career was possible under a system which was both congenial and paternal. Brutal treatment was the rare exception. Flogging still survived in the merchant service and was defended by captains otherwise humane, but a skipper, no matter how short-tempered, would be unlikely to abuse a youth whose parents might live on the same street with him and attend the same church.

The Atlantic packets brought a different order of things, which was to be continued through the clipper era. Yankee sailors showed no love for the cold and storms of the Western Ocean in these foaming packets which were remorselessly driven for speed. The masters therefore took what they could get. All the work of rigging, sail-making, scraping, painting, and keeping a ship in perfect repair was done in port instead of at sea, as was the habit in the China and California clippers, and the lore and training of the real deep-water sailor became superfluous. The crew of a packet made sail or took it in with the two-fisted mates to show them how.

From these conditions was evolved the "Liverpool packet rat," hairy and wild and drunken, the prey of crimps and dive-keepers ashore, brave and toughened to every hardship afloat, climbing aloft in his red shirt, dungaree breeches, and sea-boots, with a snow-squall whistling, the rigging sheathed with ice, and the old ship burying her bows in the thundering combers. It was the doctrine of his officers that he could not be ruled by anything short of violence, and the man to tame and hammer him was the "bucko" second mate, the test of whose fitness was that he could whip his weight in wild cats. When he became unable to maintain discipline with fists and belaying-pins, he was deposed for a better man.

Your seasoned packet rat sought the ship with a hard name by choice. His chief ambition was to kick in the ribs or pound senseless some invincible bucko mate. There was provocation enough on

both sides. Officers had to take their ships to sea
and strain every nerve to make a safe and rapid
passage with crews which were drunk and useless
when herded aboard, half of them greenhorns,
perhaps, who could neither reef nor steer. Bru-
tality was the one argument able to enforce instant
obedience among men who respected nothing else.
As a class the packet sailors became more and more
degraded because their life was intolerable to decent men. It followed therefore that the quarter-
deck employed increasing severity, and, as the
officer's authority in this respect was unchecked
and unlimited, it was easy to mistake the harshest
tyranny for wholesome discipline.

Reënforcing the bucko mate was the tradition
that the sailor was a dog, a different human species
from the landsman, without laws and usages to
protect him. This was a tradition which, for centuries, had been fostered in the naval service,
and it survived among merchant sailors as an unhappy anachronism even into the twentieth century, when an American Congress was reluctant
to bestow upon a seaman the decencies of existence enjoyed by the poorest laborer ashore.

It is in the nature of a paradox that the brilliant
success of the packet ships in dominating the

North Atlantic trade should have been a factor in the decline of the nation's maritime prestige and resources. Through a period of forty years the pride and confidence in these ships, their builders, and the men who sailed them, was intense and universal. They were a superlative product of the American genius, which still displayed the energies of a maritime race. On other oceans the situation was no less gratifying. American ships were the best and cheapest in the world. The business held the confidence of investors and commanded an abundance of capital. It was assumed, as late as 1840, that the wooden sailing ship would continue to be the supreme type of deep-water vessel because the United States possessed the greatest stores of timber, the most skillful builders and mechanics, and the ablest merchant navigators. No industry was ever more efficiently organized and conducted. American ships were most in demand and commanded the highest freights. The tonnage in foreign trade increased to a maximum of 904,476 in 1845. There was no doubt in the minds of the shrewdest merchants and owners and builders of the time that Great Britain would soon cease to be the mistress of the seas and must content herself with second place.

It was not considered ominous when, in 1838, the Admiralty had requested proposals for a steam service to America. This demand was prompted by the voyages of the *Sirius* and *Great Western*, wooden-hulled side-wheelers which thrashed along at ten knots' speed and crossed the Atlantic in fourteen to seventeen days. This was a much faster rate than the average time of the Yankee packets, but America was unperturbed and showed no interest in steam. In 1839 the British Government awarded an Atlantic mail contract, with an annual subsidy of $425,000 to Samuel Cunard and his associates, and thereby created the most famous of the Atlantic steamship companies.

Four of these liners began running in 1840 — an event which foretold the doom of the packet fleets, though the warning was almost unheeded in New York and Boston. Four years later Enoch Train was establishing a new packet line to Liverpool with the largest, finest ships built up to that time, the *Washington Irving, Anglo-American, Ocean Monarch, Anglo-Saxon,* and *Daniel Webster*. Other prominent shipping houses were expanding their service and were launching noble packets until 1853. Meanwhile the Cunard steamers were increasing in size and speed, and the service was no longer an experiment.

American capital now began to awaken from its dreams, and Edward K. Collins, managing owner of the Dramatic line of packets, determined to challenge the Cunarders at their own game. Aided by the Government to the extent of $385,000 a year as subsidy, he put afloat the four magnificent steamers, *Atlantic*, *Pacific*, *Baltic*, and *Arctic*, which were a day faster than the Cunarders in crossing, and reduced the voyage to nine and ten days. The Collins line, so auspiciously begun in 1850, and promising to give the United States the supremacy in steam which it had won under sail, was singularly unfortunate and short-lived. The *Arctic* and the *Pacific* were lost at sea, and Congress withdrew its financial support after five years. Deprived of this aid, Mr. Collins was unable to keep the enterprise afloat in competition with the subsidized Cunard fleet. In this manner and with little further effort by American interests to compete for the prize, the dominion of the Atlantic passed into British hands.

The packet ships had held on too long. It had been a stirring episode for the passengers to cheer in mid-ocean when the lofty pyramids of canvas swept grandly by some wallowing steamer and left her far astern, but in the fifties this gallant picture became less frequent, and a sooty banner of smoke on the horizon proclaimed the new era and the obliteration of all the rushing life and beauty of the tall ship under sail. Slow to realize and acknowledge defeat, persisting after the steamers were capturing the cabin passenger and express freight traffic, the American ship-owners could not visualize this profound transformation. Their majestic clippers still surpassed all rivals in the East India and China trade and were racing around the Horn, making new records for speed and winning fresh nautical triumphs for the Stars and Stripes.

This reluctance to change the industrial and commercial habits of generations of American ship-owners was one of several causes for the decadence which was hastened by the Civil War. For once the astute American was caught napping by his British cousin, who was swayed by no sentimental values and showed greater adaptability in adopting the iron steamer with the screw propeller as the inevitable successor of the wooden ship with arching topsails.

The golden age of the American merchant marine was that of the square-rigged ship, intricate, capricious, and feminine in her beauty, with forty nimble seamen in the forecastle, not that of the

metal trough with an engine in the middle and
mechanics sweating in her depths. When the Atlantic packet was compelled to abdicate, it was the
beginning of the end. After all, her master was the
fickle wind, for a slashing outward passage might
be followed by weeks of beating home to the westward. Steadily forging ahead to the beat of her
paddles or the thrash of her screw, the steamer
even of that day was far more dependable than the
sailing vessel. The *Lightning* clipper might run a
hundred miles farther in twenty-four hours than
ever a steamer had done, but she could not
maintain this meteoric burst of speed. Upon the
heaving surface of the Western Ocean there was
enacted over again the fable of the hare and the
tortoise.

Most of the famous chanteys were born in the
packet service and shouted as working choruses by
the tars of this Western Ocean before the chantey-
man perched upon a capstan and led the refrain
in the clipper trade. You will find their origin
unmistakable in such lines as these:

> As I was a-walking down Rotherhite Street,
>   'Way, ho, blow the man down;
> A pretty young creature I chanced for to meet,
>   Give me some time to blow the man down.

Soon we'll be in London City,
 Blow, boys, blow,
And see the gals all dressed so pretty,
 Blow, my bully boys, blow.

Haunting melodies, folk-song as truly as that of the plantation negro, they vanished from the sea with a breed of men who, for all their faults, possessed the valor of the Viking and the fortitude of the Spartan. Outcasts ashore — which meant to them only the dance halls of Cherry Street and the grog-shops of Ratcliffe Road — they had virtues that were as great as their failings. Across the intervening years, with a pathos indefinable, come the lovely strains of

Shenandoah, I'll ne'er forget you,
 Away, ye rolling river,
 Till the day I die I'll love you ever,
 Ah, ha, we're bound away.

CHAPTER IX

THE STATELY CLIPPER AND HER GLORY

THE American clipper ship was the result of an evolution which can be traced back to the swift privateers which were built during the War of 1812. In this type of vessel the shipyards of Chesapeake Bay excelled and their handiwork was known as the "Baltimore clipper," the name suggested by the old English verb which Dryden uses to describe the flight of the falcon that "clips it down the wind." The essential difference between the clipper ship and other kinds of merchant craft was that speed and not capacity became the chief consideration. This was a radical departure for large vessels, which in all maritime history had been designed with an eye to the number of tons they were able to carry. More finely molded lines had hitherto been found only in the much smaller French lugger, the Mediterranean galley, the American schooner.

To borrow the lines of these fleet and graceful models and apply them to the design of a deep-water ship was a bold conception. It was first attempted by Isaac McKim, a Baltimore merchant, who ordered his builders in 1832 to reproduce as closely as possible the superior sailing qualities of the renowned clipper brigs and schooners of their own port. The result was the *Ann McKim*, of nearly five hundred tons, the first Yankee clipper ship, and distinguished as such by her long, easy water-lines, low free-board, and raking stem. She was built and finished without regard to cost, copper-sheathed, the decks gleaming with brass-work and mahogany fittings. But though she was a very fast and handsome ship and the pride of her owner, the *Ann McKim* could stow so little cargo that shipping men regarded her as unprofitable and swore by their full-bodied vessels a few years longer.

That the *Ann McKim*, however, influenced the ideas of the most progressive builders is very probable, for she was later owned by the New York firm of Howland and Aspinwall, who placed an order for the first extremely sharp clipper ship of the era. This vessel, the *Rainbow*, was designed by John W. Griffeths, a marine architect, who was a pioneer in that he studied shipbuilding as a science instead of working by rule-of-thumb. The *Rainbow*, which created a sensation while on the stocks because of her concave or hollowed lines forward, which defied all tradition and practice, was launched in 1845. She was a more radical innovation than the *Ann McKim* but a successful one, for on her second voyage to China the *Rainbow* went out against the northeast monsoon in ninety-two days and came home in eighty-eight, a record which few ships were able to better. Her commander, Captain John Land, declared her to be the fastest ship in the world and there were none to dispute him.

Even the *Rainbow*, however, was eclipsed when not long afterward Howland and Aspinwall, now converted to the clipper, ordered the *Sea Witch* to be built for Captain Bob Waterman. Among all the splendid skippers of the time he was the most dashing figure. About his briny memory cluster a hundred yarns, some of them true, others legendary. It has been argued that the speed of the clippers was due more to the men who commanded them than to their hulls and rigging, and to support the theory the career of Captain Bob Waterman is quoted. He was first known to fame in the old *Natchez*, which was not a clipper at all and was even rated as slow while carrying cotton from New Orleans to New York. But Captain Bob took this full-pooped old packet ship around the Horn and employed her in the China tea trade. The voyages which he made in her were all fast, and he crowned them with the amazing run of seventy-eight days from Canton to New York, just one day behind the swiftest clipper passage ever sailed and which he himself performed in the *Sea Witch*. Incredulous mariners simply could not explain this feat of the *Natchez* and suggested that Bob Waterman must have brought the old hooker home by some new route of his own discovery.

Captain Bob had won a reputation for discipline as the mate of a Black Ball liner, a rough school, and he was not a mild man. Ashore his personality was said to have been a most attractive one, but there is no doubt that afloat he worked the very souls out of his sailors. The rumors that he frightfully abused them were not current, however, until he took the *Sea Witch* and showed the world the fastest ship under canvas. Low in the water, with black hull and gilded figurehead, she seemed too small to support her prodigious cloud of sail. For

her there were to be no leisurely voyages with
Captain Bob Waterman on the quarter-deck.
Home from Canton she sped in seventy-seven days
and then in seventy-nine — records which were
never surpassed.

With what consummate skill and daring this
master mariner drove his ship and how the race of
hardy sailors to which he belonged compared with
those of other nations may be descried in the log
of another of them, Captain Philip Dumaresq,
homeward bound from China in 1849 in the clipper
Great Britain. Three weeks out from Java Head
she had overtaken and passed seven ships heading
the same way, and then she began to rush by them
in one gale after another. Her log records her
exploits in such entries as these: "Passed a ship
under double reefs, we with our royals and studdingsails set. . . . Passed a ship laying-to under
a close-reefed maintopsail. . . . Split all three
topsails and had to heave to. . . . Seven vessels
in sight and we outsail all of them. . . . Under
double-reefed topsails passed several vessels hove-
to." Much the same record might be read in the
log of the medium clipper *Florence* — and it is
the same story of carrying sail superbly on a
ship which had been built to stand up under it:

"Passed two barks under reefed courses and close-reefed topsails standing the same way, we with royals and topgallant studding-sails," or "Passed a ship under topsails, we with our royals set." For eleven weeks "the topsail halliards were started only once, to take in a single reef for a few hours." It is not surprising, therefore, to learn that, seventeen days out from Shanghai, the *Florence* exchanged signals with the English ship *John Masterman*, which had sailed thirteen days before her.

Two notable events in the history of the nineteenth century occurred within the same year, 1849, to open new fields of trade to the Yankee clipper. One of these was the repeal of the British Navigation Laws which had given English ships a monopoly of the trade between London and the British East Indies, and the other was the discovery of gold in California. After centuries of pomp and power, the great East India Company had been deprived of its last exclusive rights afloat in 1833. Its ponderous, frigate-built merchantmen ceased to dominate the British commerce with China and India and were sold or broken up. All British ships were now free to engage in this trade, but the spirit and customs of the old régime still strongly survived. Flying the house-flags of private owners, the East Indiamen and China tea ships were still built and manned like frigates, slow, comfortable, snugging down for the night under reduced sail. There was no competition to arouse them until the last barrier of the Navigation Laws was let down and they had to meet the Yankee clipper with the tea trade as the huge stake.

Then at last it was farewell to the gallant old Indiaman and her ornate, dignified prestige. With a sigh the London *Times* confessed: "We must run a race with our gigantic and unshackled rival. We must set our long-practised skill, our steady industry, and our dogged determination against his youth, ingenuity, and ardor. Let our shipbuilders and employers take warning in time. There will always be an abundant supply of vessels good enough and fast enough for short voyages. But we want fast vessels for the long voyages which otherwise will fall into American hands."

Before English merchants could prepare themselves for these new conditions, the American clipper *Oriental* was loading in 1850 at Hong Kong with tea for the London market. Because of her reputation for speed, she received freightage of six pounds sterling per ton while British ships rode at anchor with empty holds or were glad to sail at three pounds ten per ton. Captain Theodore Palmer delivered his sixteen hundred tons of tea in the West India Docks, London, after a crack passage of ninety-one days which had never been equaled. His clipper earned $48,000, or two-thirds of what it had cost to build her. Her arrival in London created a profound impression. The port had seen nothing like her for power and speed; her skysail yards soared far above the other shipping; the cut of her snowy canvas was faultless; all clumsy, needless top-hamper had been done away with; and she appeared to be the last word in design and construction, as lean and fine and spirited as a race-horse in training.

This new competition dismayed British shipping until it could rally and fight with similar weapons. The technical journal, *Naval Science*, acknowledged that the tea trade of the London markets had passed almost out of the hands of the English ship-owner, and that British vessels, well-manned and well-found, were known to lie for weeks in the harbor of Foo-chow, waiting for a cargo and seeing American clippers come in, load, and sail immediately with full cargoes at a higher freight than they could command. Even the Government viewed the loss of trade with concern and sent admiralty draftsmen to copy the lines of the *Oriental* and *Challenge* while they were in drydock.

British clippers were soon afloat, somewhat different in model from the Yankee ships, but very fast and able, and racing them in the tea trade until the Civil War. With them it was often nip and tuck, as in the contest between the English *Lord of the Isles* and the American clipper bark *Maury* in 1856. The prize was a premium of one pound per ton for the first ship to reach London with tea of the new crop. The *Lord of the Isles* finished loading and sailed four days ahead of the *Maury*, and after thirteen thousand miles of ocean they passed Gravesend within ten minutes of each other. The British skipper, having the smartest tug and getting his ship first into dock, won the honors. In a similar race between the American *Sea Serpent* and the English *Crest of the Wave*, both ships arrived off the Isle of Wight on the same day. It was a notable fact that the *Lord of the Isles* was the first tea clipper built of iron at a date when the use of this stubborn material was not yet thought of by the men who constructed the splendid wooden ships of America.

For the peculiar requirements of the tea trade,

English maritime talent was quick to perfect a clipper type which, smaller than the great Yankee skysail-yarder, was nevertheless most admirable for its beauty and performance. On both sides of the Atlantic partizans hotly championed their respective fleets. In 1852 the American Navigation Club, organized by Boston merchants and owners, challenged the shipbuilders of Great Britain to race from a port in England to a port in China and return, for a stake of $50,000 a side, ships to be not under eight hundred nor over twelve hundred tons American register. The challenge was aimed at the *Stornaway* and the *Chrysolite*, the two clippers that were known to be the fastest ships under the British flag. Though this sporting defiance caused lively discussion, nothing came of it, and it was with a spirit even keener that Sampson and Tappan of Boston offered to match their *Nightingale* for the same amount against any clipper afloat, British or American.

In spite of the fact that Yankee enterprise had set the pace in the tea trade, within a few years after 1850 England had so successfully mastered the art of building these smaller clippers that the honors were fairly divided. The American owners were diverting their energies to the more lucrative

trade in larger ships sailing around the Horn to
San Francisco, a long road which, as a coastwise
voyage, was forbidden to foreign vessels under the
navigation laws. After the Civil War the fastest
tea clippers flew the British flag and into the seven-
ties they survived the competition of steam, racing
among themselves for the premiums awarded to
the quickest dispatch. No more of these beautiful
vessels were launched after 1869, and one by one
they vanished into other trades, overtaken by the
same fate which had befallen the Atlantic packet
and conquered by the cargo steamers which filed
through the Suez Canal.

Until 1848 San Francisco had been a drowsy
little Mexican trading-post, a huddle of adobe huts
and sheds where American ships collected hides —
vividly described in *Two Years Before the Mast*
— or a whaler called for wood and water. During the year preceding the frenzied migration of
the modern Argonauts, only two merchant ships,
one bark and one brig, sailed in through the
Golden Gate. In the twelve months following,
775 vessels cleared from Atlantic ports for San
Francisco, besides the rush from other countries,
and nearly fifty thousand passengers scrambled
ashore to dig for gold. Crews deserted their ships,

leaving them unable to go to sea again for lack of men, and in consequence a hundred of them were used as storehouses, hotels, and hospitals, or else rotted at their moorings. Sailors by hundreds jumped from the forecastle without waiting to stow the sails or receive their wages. Though offered as much as two hundred dollars a month to sign again, they jeered at the notion. Of this great fleet at San Francisco in 1849, it was a lucky ship that ever left the harbor again.

It seemed as if the whole world were bound to California and almost overnight there was created the wildest, most extravagant demand for transportation known to history. A clipper costing $70,000 could pay for herself in one voyage, with freights at sixty dollars a ton. This gold stampede might last but a little while. To take instant advantage of it was the thing. The fastest ships, and as many of them as could be built, would skim the cream of it. This explains the brief and illustrious era of the California clipper, one hundred and sixty of which were launched from 1850 to 1854. The shipyards of New York and Boston were crowded with them, and they graced the keel blocks of the historic old ports of New England — Medford, Mystic, Newburyport, Portsmouth,

Portland, Rockland, and Bath — wherever the timber and the shipwrights could be assembled.

Until that time there had been few ships afloat as large as a thousand tons. These were of a new type, rapidly increased to fifteen hundred, two thousand tons, and over. They presented new and difficult problems in spars and rigging able to withstand the strain of immense areas of canvas which climbed two hundred feet to the skysail pole and which, with lower studdingsails set, spread one hundred and sixty feet from boom-end to boom-end. There had to be the strength to battle with the furious tempests of Cape Horn and at the same time the driving power to sweep before the sweet and steadfast trade-winds. Such a queenly clipper was the *Flying Cloud*, the achievement of that master builder, Donald McKay, which sailed from New York to San Francisco in eighty-nine days, with Captain Josiah Creesy in command. This record was never lowered and was equaled only twice — by the *Flying Cloud* herself and by the *Andrew Jackson* nine years later. It was during this memorable voyage that the *Flying Cloud* sailed 1256 miles in four days while steering to the northward under topgallantsails after rounding Cape Horn. This was a rate of speed which, if sustained, would have carried her from New York to Queenstown in eight days and seventeen hours. This speedy passage was made in 1851, and only two years earlier the record for the same voyage of fifteen thousand miles had been one hundred and twenty days, by the clipper *Memnon*.

Donald McKay now resolved to build a ship larger and faster than the *Flying Cloud*, and his genius neared perfection in the *Sovereign of the Seas*, of 2421 tons' register, which exceeded in size all merchant vessels afloat. This Titan of the clipper fleet was commanded by Donald's brother, Captain Lauchlan McKay, with a crew of one hundred and five men and boys. During her only voyage to San Francisco she was partly dismasted; but Lauchlan McKay rigged her anew at sea in fourteen days and still made port in one hundred and three days, a record for the season of the year.

It was while running home from Honolulu in 1853 that the *Sovereign of the Seas* realized the hopes of her builder. In eleven days she sailed 3562 miles, with four days logged for a total of 1478 knots. Making allowance for the longitudes and difference in time, this was an average daily run of 378 sea miles or 435 land miles. Using the same comparison, the distance from Sandy Hook to Queenstown would have been covered in seven days and nine hours. Figures are arid reading, perhaps, but these are wet by the spray and swept by the salt winds of romance. During one of these four days the *Sovereign of the Seas* reeled off 424 nautical miles, during which her average speed was seventeen and two-thirds knots and at times reached nineteen and twenty. The only sailing ship which ever exceeded this day's work was the *Lightning*, built later by the same Donald McKay, which ran 436 knots in the Atlantic passage already referred to. The *Sovereign of the Seas* could also boast of a sensational feat upon the Western Ocean, for between New York and Liverpool she outsailed the Cunard liner *Canada* by 325 miles in five days.

It is curiously interesting to notice that the California clipper era is almost generally ignored by the foremost English writers of maritime history. For one thing, it was a trade in which their own ships were not directly concerned, and partizan bias is apt to color the views of the best of us when national prestige is involved. American historians themselves have dispensed with many unpleasant facts when engaged with the War of 1812. With regard to the speed of clipper ships, however, involving a rivalry far more thrilling and important than all the races ever sailed for the *America's* cup, the evidence is available in concrete form.

Lindsay's *History of Merchant Shipping* is the most elaborate English work of the kind. Heavily ballasted with facts and rather dull reading for the most part, it kindles with enthusiasm when eulogizing the *Thermopylæ* and the *Sir Launcelot*, composite clippers of wood and iron, afloat in 1870, which it declares to be "the fastest sailing ships that ever traversed the ocean." This fairly presents the issue which a true-blooded Yankee has no right to evade. The greatest distance sailed by the *Sir Launcelot* in twenty-four hours between China and London was 354 knots, compared with the 424 miles of the *Sovereign of the Seas* and the 436 miles of the *Lightning*. Her best sustained run was one of seven days for an average of a trifle more than 300 miles a day. Against this is to be recorded the performance of the *Sovereign of the Seas*, 3562 miles in eleven days, at the rate of 324 miles every twenty-four hours, and her wonderful four-day run of 1478 miles, an average of 378 miles.

The *Thermopylæ* achieved her reputation in a passage of sixty-three days from London to Melbourne — a record which was never beaten. Her fastest day's sailing was 330 miles, or not quite sixteen knots an hour. In six days she traversed 1748 miles, an average of 291 miles a day. In this Australian trade the American clippers made little effort to compete. Those engaged in it were mostly built for English owners and sailed by British skippers, who could not reasonably be expected to get the most out of these loftily sparred Yankee ships, which were much larger than their own vessels of the same type. The *Lightning* showed what she could do from Melbourne to Liverpool by making the passage in sixty-three days, with 3722 miles in ten consecutive days and one day's sprint of 412 miles.

In the China tea trade the *Thermopylæ* drove home from Foo-chow in ninety-one days, which was equaled by the *Sir Launcelot*. The American *Witch of the Wave* had a ninety-day voyage to her credit, and the *Comet* ran from Liverpool to Shanghai in eighty-four days. Luck was a larger factor on this route than in the California or Australian trade because of the fitful uncertainty of the monsoons, and as a test of speed it was rather unsatisfactory. In a very fair-minded and expert summary, Captain Arthur H. Clark,[1] in his youth an

[1] *The Clipper Ship Era.* N. Y., 1910.

officer on Yankee clippers, has discussed this question of rival speed and power under sail — a question which still absorbs those who love the sea. His conclusion is that in ordinary weather at sea, when great power to carry sail was not required, the British tea clippers were extremely fast vessels, chiefly on account of their narrow beam. Under these conditions they were perhaps as fast as the American clippers of the same class, such as the *Sea Witch*, *White Squall*, *Northern Light*, and *Sword-Fish*. But if speed is to be reckoned by the maximum performance of a ship under the most favorable conditions, then the British tea clippers were certainly no match for the larger American ships such as the *Flying Cloud*, *Sovereign of the Seas*, *Hurricane*, *Trade Wind*, *Typhoon*, *Flying Fish*, *Challenge*, and *Red Jacket*. The greater breadth of the American ships in proportion to their length meant power to carry canvas and increased buoyancy which enabled them, with their sharper ends, to be driven in strong gales and heavy seas at much greater speed than the British clippers. The latter were seldom of more than one thousand tons' register and combined in a superlative degree the good qualities of merchant ships.

It was the California trade, brief and crowded

and fevered, which saw the roaring days of the
Yankee clipper and which was familiar with racing
surpassing in thrill and intensity that of the packet
ships of the Western Ocean. In 1851, for instance,
the *Raven*, *Sea Witch*, and *Typhoon* sailed for San
Francisco within the same week. They crossed
the Equator a day apart and stood away to the
southward for three thousand miles of the south-
east trades and the piping westerly winds which
prevailed farther south. At fifty degrees south
latitude the *Raven* and the *Sea Witch* were abeam
of each other with the *Typhoon* only two days
astern.

Now they stripped for the tussle to windward
around Cape Horn, sending down studdingsail
booms and skysail yards, making all secure with
extra lashings, plunging into the incessant head
seas of the desolate ocean, fighting it out tack for
tack, reefing topsails and shaking them out again,
the vigilant commanders going below only to
change their clothes, the exhausted seamen stub-
bornly, heroically handling with frozen, bleeding
fingers the icy sheets and canvas. A fortnight of
this inferno and the *Sea Witch* and the *Raven*
gained the Pacific, still within sight of each other,
and the *Typhoon* only one day behind. Then

they swept northward, blown by the booming trade-winds, spreading studdingsails, skysails, and above them, like mere handkerchiefs, the water-sails and ring-tails. Again the three clippers crossed the Equator. Close-hauled on the starboard tack, their bowsprits were pointed for the last stage of the journey to the Golden Gate. The *Typhoon* now overhauled her rivals and was the first to signal her arrival, but the victory was earned by the *Raven*, which had set her departure from Boston Light while the others had sailed from New York. The *Typhoon* and the *Raven* were only a day apart, with the *Sea Witch* five days behind the leader.

Clipper ship crews included men of many nations. In the average forecastle there would be two or three Americans, a majority of English and Norwegians, and perhaps a few Portuguese and Italians. The hardiest seamen, and the most un-manageable, were the Liverpool packet rats who were lured from their accustomed haunts to join the clippers by the magical call of the gold-diggings. There were not enough deep-water sailors to man half the ships that were built in these few years, and the crimps and boarding-house runners decoyed or flung aboard on sailing day as many men as were demanded, and any drunken, broken landlubber was good enough to be shipped as an able seaman. They were things of rags and tatters — their only luggage a bottle of whiskey.

The mates were thankful if they could muster enough real sailors to work the ship to sea and then began the stern process of whipping the wastrels and incompetents into shape for the perils and emergencies of the long voyage. That these great clippers were brought safely to port is a shining tribute to the masterful skill of their officers. While many of them were humane and just, with all their severity, the stories of savage abuse which are told of some are shocking in the extreme. The defense was that it was either mutiny or club the men under. Better treatment might have persuaded better men to sail. Certain it is that life in the forecastle of a clipper was even more intolerable to the self-respecting American youth than it had previously been aboard the Atlantic packet.

When Captain Bob Waterman arrived at San Francisco in the *Challenge* clipper in 1851, a mob tried very earnestly to find and hang him and his officers because of the harrowing stories told by his sailors. That he had shot several of them from the yards with his pistol to make the others move faster was one count in the indictment. For his part, Captain Waterman asserted that a more desperate crew of ruffians had never sailed out of New York and that only two of them were Americans. They were mutinous from the start, half of them blacklegs of the vilest type who swore to get the upper hand of him. His mates, boatswain, and carpenter had broken open their chests and boxes and had removed a collection of slung-shots, knuckle-dusters, bowie-knives, and pistols. Off Rio Janeiro they had tried to kill the chief mate, and Captain Waterman had been compelled to jump in and stretch two of them dead with an iron belaying-pin. Off Cape Horn three sailors fell from aloft and were lost. This accounted for the casualties.

The truth of such episodes as these was difficult to fathom. Captain Waterman demanded a legal investigation, but nothing came of his request and he was commended by his owners for his skill and courage in bringing the ship to port without losing a spar or a sail. It was a skipper of this old school who blandly maintained the doctrine that if you wanted the men to love you, you must starve them and knock them down. The fact is proven by scores of cases that the discipline of the American clipper was both famously efficient and notoriously cruel. It was not until long after American sailors had ceased to exist that adequate legislation was enacted to provide that they should be treated as human beings afloat and ashore. Other days and other customs! It is perhaps unkind to judge these vanished master-mariners too harshly, for we cannot comprehend the crises which continually beset them in their command.

No more extreme clipper ships were built after 1854. The California frenzy had subsided and speed in carrying merchandise was no longer so essential; besides, the passenger traffic was seeking the Isthmian route. What were called medium clippers enjoyed a profitable trade for many years later, and one of them, the *Andrew Jackson*, was never outsailed for the record from New York to San Francisco. This splendid type of ship was to be found on every sea, for the United States was still a commanding factor in the maritime activities of South America, India, China, Europe, and Australia. In 1851 its merchant tonnage rivaled that of England and was everywhere competing with it.

The effects of the financial panic of 1857 and the

aftermath of business depression were particularly disastrous to American ships. Freights were so low as to yield no profit, and the finest clippers went begging for charters. The yards ceased to launch new tonnage. British builders had made such rapid progress in design and construction that the days of Yankee preference in the China trade had passed. The Stars and Stripes floated over ships waiting idle in Manila Bay, at Shanghai, Hong-Kong, and Calcutta. The tide of commerce had slackened abroad as well as at home and the surplus of deep-water tonnage was world-wide.

In earlier generations afloat, the American spirit had displayed amazing recuperative powers. The havoc of the Revolution had been unable to check it, and its vigor and aggressive enterprise had never been more notable than after the blows dealt by the Embargo, the French Spoliations, and the War of 1812. The conditions of trade and the temper of the people were now so changed that this mighty industry, aforetime so robust and resilient, was unable to recover from such shocks as the panic of 1857 and the Civil War. Yet it had previously survived and triumphed over calamities far more severe. The destruction wrought by Confederate cruisers was trifling compared with the

work of the British and French privateers when
the nation was very small and weak.

The American spirit had ceased to concern itself
with the sea as the vital and dominant element.
The footsteps of the young men no longer turned
toward the wharf and the waterside and the tiers of
tall ships outward bound. They were aspiring to
conquer an inland empire of prairie and mountain
and desert, impelled by the same pioneering and
adventurous ardor which had burned in their
seafaring sires. Steam had vanquished sail — an
epochal event in a thousand years of maritime
history — but the nation did not care enough to
accept this situation as a new challenge or to continue the ancient struggle for supremacy upon the
sea. England did care, because it was life or death
to the little, sea-girt island, but as soon as the
United States ceased to be a strip of Atlantic seaboard and the panorama of a continent was un-
rolled to settlement, it was foreordained that the
maritime habit of thought and action should lose
its virility in America. All great seafaring races,
English, Norwegian, Portuguese, and Dutch, have
taken to salt water because there was lack of space,
food, or work ashore, and their strong young men
craved opportunities. Like the Pilgrim Fathers

and their fishing shallops they had nowhere else to go.

When the *Flying Cloud* and the clippers of her kind — taut, serene, immaculate — were sailing through the lonely spaces of the South Atlantic and the Pacific, they sighted now and then the stumpy, slatternly rig and greasy hull of a New Bedford whaler, perhaps rolling to the weight of a huge carcass alongside. With a poor opinion of the seamanship of these wandering barks, the clipper crews rolled out, among their favorite chanteys:

> Oh, poor Reuben Ranzo,
> Ranzo, boys, O Ranzo,
> Oh, Ranzo was no sailor,
> So they shipped him aboard a whaler,
> Ranzo, boys, O Ranzo.

This was crass, intolerant prejudice. The whaling ship was careless of appearances, it is true, and had the air of an ocean vagabond; but there were other duties more important than holystoning decks, scraping spars, and trimming the yards to a hair. On a voyage of two or three years, moreover, there was always plenty of time tomorrow. Brave and resourceful seamen were these New England adventurers and deep-sea hunters who made nautical history after their own fashion. They flourished coeval with the merchant marine in its prime, and they passed from the sea at about the same time and for similar reasons. Modernity dispensed with their services, and young men found elsewhere more profitable and easier employment.

The great days of Nantucket as a whaling port were passed before the Revolution wiped out her ships and killed or scattered her sailors. It was later discovered that larger ships were more economical, and Nantucket harbor bar was too shoal to admit their passage. For this reason New Bedford became the scene of the foremost activity, and Nantucket thereafter played a minor part, although her barks went cruising on to the end of the chapter and her old whaling families were true to strain. As explorers the whalemen rambled into every nook and corner of the Pacific before merchant vessels had found their way thither. They discovered uncharted islands and cheerfully fought savages or suffered direful shipwreck. The chase led them into Arctic regions where their stout barks were nipped like eggshells among the grinding floes, or else far to the southward where they broiled in tropic calms. The New Bedford lad was as keen to go a-whaling as was his counterpart in Boston or New York to be the dandy mate of a California clipper, and true was the song:

> I asked a maiden by my side,
> Who sighed and looked to me forlorn,
>   "Where is your heart?" She quick replied,
> "Round Cape Horn."

Yankee whaling reached its high tide in 1857 when the New Bedford fleet alone numbered 329 sail and those owned in other ports of Buzzard's Bay swelled the total to 426 vessels, besides thirty more hailing from New London and Sag Harbor. In this year the value of the catch was more than ten million dollars. The old custom of sailing on shares or "lays" instead of wages was never changed. It was win or lose for all hands — now a handsome fortune or again an empty hold and pockets likewise. There was Captain W. T. Walker of New Bedford who, in 1847, bought for a song a ship so old that she was about to be broken up for junk and no insurance broker would look at her. In this rotten relic he shipped a crew and went sailing in the Pacific. Miraculously keeping afloat, this *Envoy* of his was filled to the hatches with oil and bones, twice running, before she returned to her home port; and she earned $138,450 on a total investment of eight thousand dollars.

The ship *Sarah* of Nantucket, after a three years' cruise, brought back 3497 barrels of sperm oil which sold for $89,000, and the *William Hamilton* of New Bedford set another high mark by stowing 4181 barrels of a value of $109,269. The *Pioneer* of New London, Captain Ebenezer Morgan, was away only a year and stocked a cargo of oil and whalebone which sold for $150,060. Most of the profits of prosperous voyages were taken as the owners' share, and the incomes of the captain and crew were so niggardly as to make one wonder why they persisted in a calling so perilous, arduous, and poorly paid. During the best years of whaling, when the ships were averaging $16,000 for a voyage, the master received an eighteenth, or about nine hundred dollars a year. The highly skilled hands, such as the boat-steerers and harpooners, had a lay of only one seventy-fifth, or perhaps a little more than two hundred dollars cash as the reward of a voyage which netted the owner at least fifty per cent on his investment. Occasionally they fared better than this and sometimes worse. The answer to the riddle is that they liked the life and had always the gambling spirit which hopes for a lucky turn of the cards.

The countless episodes of fragile boats smashed

to kindling by fighting whales, of the attack renewed with harpoon and lance, of ships actually rammed and sunk, would fill a volume by themselves and have been stirringly narrated in many a one. Zanzibar and Kamchatka, Tasmania and the Seychelles knew the lean, sun-dried Yankee whaleman and his motto of a "dead whale or a stove boat." The Civil War did not drive him from the seas. The curious fact is that his products commanded higher prices in 1907 than fifty years before, but the number of his ships rapidly decreased. Whales were becoming scarce, and New England capital preferred other forms of investment. The leisurely old sailing craft was succeeded by the steam whaler, and the explosive bomb slew, instead of the harpoon and lance hurled by the sinewy right arm of a New Bedford man or Cape Verde islander.

Roving whaler and armed East Indiaman, plunging packet ship and stately clipper, they served their appointed days and passed on their several courses to become mere memories, as shadowy and unsubstantial as the gleam of their own topsails when seen at twilight. The souls of their sailors have fled to Fiddler's Green, where all dead mariners go. They were of the old merchant marine which contributed something fine and imperishable to the story of the United States. Down the wind, vibrant and deep-throated, comes their own refrain for a requiem:

> We're outward bound this very day,
> Good-bye, fare you well,
> Good-bye, fare you well.
> We're outward bound this very day,
>   Hurrah, my boys, we're outward bound.

CHAPTER X

BOUND COASTWISE

ONE thinks of the old merchant marine in terms of the clipper ship and distant ports. The coasting trade has been overlooked in song and story; yet, since the year 1859, its fleets have always been larger and more important than the American deep-water commerce nor have decay and misfortune overtaken them. It is a traffic which flourished from the beginning, ingeniously adapting itself to new conditions, unchecked by war, and surviving with splendid vigor, under steam and sail, in this modern era.

The seafaring pioneers won their way from port to port of the tempestuous Atlantic coast in tiny ketches, sloops, and shallops when the voyage of five hundred miles from New England to Virginia was a prolonged and hazardous adventure. Fog and shoals and lee shores beset these coastwise sailors, and shipwrecks were pitifully frequent.

185

In no Hall of Fame will you find the name of Captain Andrew Robinson of Gloucester, but he was nevertheless an illustrious benefactor and deserves a place among the most useful Americans. His invention was the Yankee schooner of fore-and-aft rig, and he gave to this type of vessel its name.[1] Seaworthy, fast, and easily handled, adapted for use in the early eighteenth century when inland transportation was almost impossible, the schooner carried on trade between the colonies and was an important factor in the growth of the fisheries.

Before the Revolution the first New England schooners were beating up to the Grand Bank of Newfoundland after cod and halibut. They were of no more than fifty tons' burden, too small for their task but manned by fishermen of surpassing hardihood. Marblehead was then the foremost fishing port with two hundred brigs and schooners on the offshore banks. But to Gloucester belongs the glory of sending the first schooner to the Grand Bank.[2] From these two rock-bound harbors went thousands of trained seamen to man the privateers

[1] It is said that as the odd two-master slid gracefully into the water, a spectator exclaimed: "See how she scoons!" "Aye," answered Captain Robinson, "a *schooner* let her be!" This launching took place in 1713 or 1714.

[2] Marvin's *American Merchant Marine*, p. 287.

and the ships of the Continental navy, slinging their hammocks on the gun-decks beside the whale-men of Nantucket. These fishermen and coast-wise sailors fought on the land as well and followed the drums of Washington's armies until the final scene at Yorktown. Gloucester and Marblehead were filled with widows and orphans, and half their men-folk were dead or missing.

The fishing-trade soon prospered again, and the men of the old ports tenaciously clung to the sea even when the great migration flowed westward to people the wilderness and found a new American empire. They were fishermen from father to son, bound together in an intimate community of interests, a race of pure native or English stock, deserving this tribute which was paid to them in Congress: "Every person on board our fishing vessels has an interest in common with his associates; their reward depends upon their industry and enterprise. Much caution is observed in the selection of the crews of our fishing vessels; it often happens that every individual is connected by blood and the strongest ties of friendship; our fishermen are remarkable for their sobriety and good conduct, and they rank with the most skillful navigators."

Fishing and the coastwise merchant trade were closely linked. Schooners loaded dried cod as well as lumber for southern ports and carried back naval stores and other southern products. Well-to-do fishermen owned trading vessels and sent out their ventures, the sailors shifting from one forecastle to the other. With a taste for an easier life than the stormy, freezing Banks, the young Gloucester- man would sign on for a voyage to Pernambuco or Havana and so be fired with ambition to become a mate or master and take to deep water after a while. In this way was maintained a school of seamanship which furnished the most intelligent and efficient officers of the merchant marine. For generations they were mostly recruited from the old fishing and shipping ports of New England until the term "Yankee shipmaster" had a mean- ing peculiarly its own.

Seafaring has undergone so many revolutionary changes and old days and ways are so nearly ob- literated that it is singular to find the sailing ves- sel still employed in great numbers, even though the gasolene motor is being installed to kick her along in spells of calm weather. The Gloucester fishing schooner, perfect of her type, stanch, fleet, and powerful, still drives homeward from the Banks under a tall press of canvas, and her crew still divide the earnings, share and share, as did their forefathers a hundred and fifty years ago. But the old New England strain of blood no longer predominates, and Portuguese, Scandinavians, and Nova Scotia "Blue-noses" bunk with the lads of Gloucester stock. Yet they are alike for courage, hardihood, and mastery of the sea, and the traditions of the calling are undimmed.

There was a time before the Civil War when Congress jealously protected the fisheries by means of a bounty system and legislation aimed against our Canadian neighbors. The fishing fleets were regarded as a source of national wealth and the nursery of prime seamen for the navy and merchant marine. In 1858 the bounty system was abandoned, however, and the fishermen were left to shift for themselves, earning small profits at peril of their lives and preferring to follow the sea because they knew no other profession. In spite of this loss of assistance from the Government, the tonnage engaged in deep-sea fisheries was never so great as in the second year of the Civil War. Four years later the industry had shrunk one-half; and it has never recovered its early importance.[1]

[1] In 1862, the tonnage amounted to 193,459; in 1866, to 89,386.

The coastwise merchant trade, on the other hand, has been jealously guarded against competition and otherwise fostered ever since 1789, when the first discriminatory tonnage tax was enforced. The Embargo Act of 1808 prohibited domestic commerce to foreign flags, and this edict was renewed in the American Navigation Act of 1817. It remained a firmly established doctrine of maritime policy until the Great War compelled its suspension as an emergency measure. The theories of protection and free trade have been bitterly debated for generations, but in this instance the practice was eminently successful and the results were vastly impressive. Deep-water shipping dwindled and died, but the increase in coastwise sailing was consistent. It rose to five million tons early in this century and makes the United States still one of the foremost maritime powers in respect to salt-water activity.

To speak of this deep-water shipping as trade coastwise is misleading, in a way. The words convey an impression of dodging from port to port for short distances, whereas many of the voyages are longer than those of the foreign routes in European waters. It is farther by sea from Boston to Philadelphia than from Plymouth, England, to Bordeaux.

A schooner making the run from Portland to Savannah lays more knots over her stern than a tramp bound out from England to Lisbon. It is a shorter voyage from Cardiff to Algiers than an American skipper pricks off on his chart when he takes his steamer from New York to New Orleans or Galveston. This coastwise trade may lack the romance of the old school of the square-rigged ship in the Roaring Forties, but it has always been the more perilous and exacting. Its seamen suffer hardships unknown elsewhere, for they have to endure winters of intense cold and heavy gales and they are always in risk of stranding or being driven ashore.

The story of these hardy men is interwoven, for the most part, with the development of the schooner in size and power. This graceful craft, so peculiar to its own coast and people, was built for utility and possessed a simple beauty of its own when under full sail. The schooners were at first very small because it was believed that large fore-and-aft sails could not be handled with safety. They were difficult to reef or lower in a blow until it was discovered that three masts instead of two made the task much easier. For many years the three-masted schooner was the most popular kind of American merchant vessel. They clustered in every Atlantic port and were built in the yards of New England, New York, New Jersey, and Virginia, — built by the mile, as the saying was, and sawed off in lengths to suit the owners' pleasure. They carried the coal, ice, lumber of the whole seaboard and were so economical of man-power that they earned dividends where steamers or square-rigged ships would not have paid for themselves.

As soon as a small steam-engine was employed to hoist the sails, it became possible to launch much larger schooners and to operate them at a marvelously low cost. Rapidly the four-master gained favor, and then came the five- and six-masted vessels, gigantic ships of their kind. Instead of the hundred-ton schooner of a century ago, Hampton Roads and Boston Harbor saw these great cargo carriers which could stow under hatches four and five thousand tons of coal, and whose masts soared a hundred and fifty feet above the deck. Square-rigged ships of the same capacity would have required crews of a hundred men, but these schooners were comfortably handled by a company of fifteen all told, only ten of whom were in the forecastle. There was no need of sweating and hauling at braces and halliards. The steam-winch undertook all this toil. The tremendous sails, stretching a hundred feet from boom to gaff could not have been managed otherwise. Even for trimming sheets or setting topsails, it was necessary merely to take a turn or two around the drum of the winch engine and turn the steam valve. The big schooner was the last word in cheap, efficient transportation by water. In her own sphere of activity she was as notable an achievement as the Western Ocean packet or the Cape Horn clipper.

The masters who sailed these extraordinary vessels also changed and had to learn a new kind of seamanship. They must be very competent men, for the tests of their skill and readiness were really greater than those demanded of the deepwater skipper. They drove these great schooners alongshore winter and summer, across Nantucket Shoals and around Cape Cod, and their salvation depended on shortening sail ahead of the gale. Let the wind once blow and the sea get up, and it was almost impossible to strip the canvas off an unwieldy six-master. The captain's chief fear was of being blown offshore, of having his vessel run away with him! Unlike the deep-water man, he preferred running in toward the beach and letting go his anchors. There he would ride out the storm and hoist sail when the weather moderated.

These were American shipmasters of the old breed, raised in schooners as a rule, and adapting themselves to modern conditions. They sailed for nominal wages and primage, or five per cent of the gross freight paid the vessel. Before the Great War in Europe, freights were low and the schooner skippers earned scanty incomes. Then came a world shortage of tonnage and immediately coastwise freights soared skyward. The big schooners of the Palmer fleet began to reap fabulous dividends and their masters shared in the unexpected opulence. Besides their primage they owned shares in their vessels, a thirty-second or so, and presently their settlement at the end of a voyage coastwise amounted to an income of a thousand dollars a month. They earned this money, and the managing owners cheerfully paid them, for there had been lean years and uncomplaining service and the sailor had proved himself worthy of his hire. So tempting was the foreign war trade, that a fleet of them was sent across the Atlantic until the American Government barred them from the war zone as too easy a prey for submarine attack. They therefore returned to the old coastwise route or loaded for South American ports — singularly interesting ships because they were the last bold venture of the old American maritime spirit, a challenge to the Age of Steam.

No more of these huge, towering schooners have been built in the last dozen years. Steam colliers and barges have won the fight because time is now more valuable than cheapness of transportation. The schooner might bowl down to Norfolk from Boston or Portland in four days and be threshing about for two weeks in head winds on the return voyage.

The small schooner appeared to be doomed somewhat earlier. She had ceased to be profitable in competition with the larger, more modern fore-and-after, but these battered, veteran craft died hard. They harked back to a simpler age, to the era of the stage-coach and the spinning-wheel, to the little shipyards that were to be found on every bay and inlet of New England. They were still owned and sailed by men who ashore were friends and neighbors. Even now you may find during your summer wanderings some stumpy, weather-worn two-master running in for shelter overnight, which has plied up and down the coast for fifty or sixty years, now leaking like a basket and too frail for winter voyages. It was in a craft very much like this that your rude ancestors went privateering against the British. Indeed, the little schooner *Polly*, which fought briskly in the War of 1812, is still afloat and loading cargoes in New England ports.

These little coasters, surviving long after the stately merchant marine had vanished from blue water, have enjoyed a slant of favoring fortune in recent years. They, too, have been in demand, and once again there is money to spare for paint and cordage and calking. They have been granted a new lease of life and may be found moored at the wharfs, beached on the marine railways, or anchored in the stream, eagerly awaiting their turn to refit. It is a matter of vital concern that the freight on spruce boards from Bangor to New York has increased to five dollars a thousand feet. Many of these craft belong to grandfatherly skippers who dared not venture past Cape Cod in December, lest the venerable *Matilda Emerson* or the valetudinarian *Joshua R. Coggswell* should open up and founder in a blow. During the winter storms these skippers used to hug the kitchen stove in bleak farmhouses until spring came and they could put to sea again. The rigor of circumstances, however,

forced others to seek for trade the whole year
through. In a recent winter fifty-seven schooners
were lost on the New England coast, most of which
were unfit for anything but summer breezes. As
by a miracle, others have been able to renew
their youth, to replace spongy planking and rotten stems, and to deck themselves out in white
canvas and fresh paint!

The captains of these craft foregather in the
ship-chandler's shops, where the floor is strewn
with sawdust, the armchairs are capacious, and
the environment harmonizes with the tales that
are told. It is an informal club of coastwise skippers and the old energy begins to show itself once
more. They move with a brisker gait than when
times were so hard and they went begging for
charters at any terms. A sinewy patriarch stumps
to a window, flourishes his arm at an ancient two-
master, and booms out:

"That vessel of mine is as sound as a nut, I tell
ye. She ain't as big as some, but I'd like nothin'
better than to fill her full of suthin' for the west
coast of Africy, same as the *Horace M. Bickford*
that cleared t'other day, stocked for *sixty thousand
dollars*."

"Huh, you'd get lost out o' sight of land, John,"

is the cruel retort, "and that old shoe-box of yours
'ud be scared to death without a harbor to run into
every time the sun clouded over. Expect to navi-
gate to Africy with an alarm-clock and a soundin'-
lead, I presume."

"Mebbe I'd better let well enough alone," re-
plies the old man. "Africy don't seem as neigh-
borly as Phippsburg and Machiasport. I'll chance
it as far as Philadelphy next voyage and I guess
the old woman can buy a new dress."

The activity and the reawakening of the old
shipyards, their slips all filled with the frames of
wooden vessels for the foreign trade, is like a revival of the old merchant marine, a reincarnation
of ghostly memories. In mellowed dignity the
square white houses beneath the New England
elms recall to mind the mariners who dwelt there-
in. It seems as if their shipyards also belonged to
the past; but the summer visitor finds a fresh
attraction in watching the new schooners rise from
the stocks, and the gay pageant of launching them,
every mast ablaze with bunting, draws crowds to
the water-front. And as a business venture, with
somewhat of the tang of old-fashioned romance,
the casual stranger is now and then tempted to
purchase a sixty-fourth "piece" of a splendid

Yankee four-master and keep in touch with its roving fortunes. The shipping reports of the daily newspaper prove more fascinating than the ticker tape, and the tidings of a successful voyage thrill one with a sense of personal gratification. For the sea has not lost its magic and its mystery, and those who go down to it in ships must still battle against elemental odds — still carry on the noble and enduring traditions of the Old Merchant Marine.

BIBLIOGRAPHICAL NOTE

As a rule, American historians like McMaster, Adams, and Rhodes give too little space to the maritime achievements of the nation. The gap has been partially filled by the following special works:

Winthrop L. Marvin, *The American Merchant Marine: Its History and Romance from 1620 to 1902* (1902). This is the most nearly complete volume of its kind by an author who knows the subject and handles it with accuracy.

John R. Spears, *The Story of the American Merchant Marine* (1910), *The American Slave Trade* (1901), *The Story of the New England Whalers* (1908). Mr. Spears has sought original sources for much of his material and his books are worth reading, particularly his history of the slave-trade.

Ralph D. Paine, *The Ships and Sailors of Old Salem: The Record of a Brilliant Era of American Achievement* (1912). A history of the most famous seaport of the Atlantic coast, drawn from log-books and other manuscript collections. *The Book of Buried Treasure: Being a True History of the Gold, Jewels, and Plate of Pirates, Galleons, etc.* (1911). Several chapters have to do with certain picturesque pirates and seamen of the colonies.

Edgar S. Maclay, *A History of American Privateers* (1899). The only book of its kind, and indispensable to those who wish to learn the story of Yankee ships and sailors.

J. R. Hutchinson, *The Press Gang Afloat and Ashore* (1914). This recent volume, written from an English point of view, illuminates the system of conscription which caused the War of 1812.

Nothing can take the place, however, of the narratives of those master mariners who made the old merchant marine famous:

Richard Henry Dana, Jr., *Two Years Before the Mast* (1840). The latest edition, handsomely illustrated, (1915). The classic narrative of American forecastle life in the sailing-ship era.

Captain Richard Cleveland, *Narrative of Voyages and Commercial Enterprises* (1842). This is one of the fascinating autobiographies of the old school of shipmasters who had the gift of writing.

Captain Amasa Delano, *Narrative of Voyages and Travels* (1817). Another of the rare human documents of blue water. It describes the most adventurous period of activity, a century ago.

Captain Arthur H. Clark, *The Clipper Ship Era* (1910). A thrilling, spray-swept, true story. Far and away the best account of the clipper, by a man who was an officer of one in his youth.

Robert Bennet Forbes, *Notes on Ships of the Past* (1888). Random facts and memories of a famous Boston ship-owner. It is valuable for its records of noteworthy passages.

Captain John D. Whidden, *Ocean Life in the Old Sailing Ship Days* (1908). The entertaining reminiscences of a veteran shipmaster.

Captain A. W. Nelson, *Yankee Swanson: Chapters*

from a Life at Sea (1913). Another of the true romances, recommended for a lively sense of humor and a faithful portrayal of life aboard a windjammer.

There are many other personal narratives, some of them privately printed and very old, which may be found in the libraries. Typical of them is *A Journal of the Travels and Sufferings of Daniel Saunders* (1794), in which a young sailor relates his adventures after shipwreck on the coast of Arabia.

Among general works the following are valuable:

J. Grey Jewell, *Among Our Sailors* (1874). A plea for more humane treatment of American seamen, with many instances on shocking brutalities as reported to the author, who was a United States Consul.

E. Keble Chatterton, *Sailing Ships: The Story of their Development* (1909). An elaborate history of the development of the sailing vessel from the earliest times to the modern steel clipper.

W. S. Lindsay, *History of Merchant Shipping and Ancient Commerce*, 4 vols. (1874–76). An English work, notably fair to the American marine, and considered authoritative.

Douglas Owen, *Ocean Trade and Shipping* (1914). An English economist explains the machinery of maritime trade and commerce.

William Wood, *All Afloat.* In *The Chronicles of Canada Series.* Glasgow, Brook and Co., Toronto, 1914.

J. B. McMaster, *The Life and Times of Stephen Girard, Mariner and Merchant*, 2 vols. (1918).

The relation of governmental policy to the merchant marine is discussed by various writers:

David A. Wells, *Our Merchant Marine: How It Rose.*

Increased, Became Great, Declined, and Decayed (1882). A political treatise in defense of a protective policy.

William A. Bates, *American Marine: The Shipping Question in History and Politics* (1892); *American Navigation: The Political History of Its Rise and Ruin* (1902). These works are statistical and highly technical, partly compiled from governmental reports, and are also frankly controversial.

Henry Hall, *American Navigation, With Some Account of the Causes of Its Former Prosperity and Present Decline* (1878).

Charles S. Hill, *History of American Shipping: Its Prestige, Decline, and Prospect* (1883).

J. D. J. Kelley, *The Question of Ships: The Navy and the Merchant Marine* (1884).

Arthur J. Maginnis, *The Atlantic Ferry: Its Ships, Men, and Working* (1900).

A vast amount of information is to be found in the Congressional Report of the Merchant Marine Commission, published in three volumes (1905).

INDEX

205